RAIN IN A DRY LAND

RAIN IN
A DRY LAND

John Knight

HODDER AND STOUGHTON
LONDON SYDNEY AUCKLAND TORONTO

'I will be to the people of Israel
like rain in a dry land'
(Hosea 14:5, Good News Bible).

British Library Cataloguing in Publication Data
A record for this book is available from the British Library

ISBN 0 340 41589 4

Printed and bound in Great Britain by
Clays Ltd, St Ives plc

Photoset by Rowland Phototypesetting Ltd,
Bury St Edmunds, Suffolk

Hodder and Stoughton Ltd
A Division of Hodder Headline PLC
338 Euston Road
London NW1 3BH

FOREWORD
by Michael Cassidy

If you are a candidate for spiritual adventure, then John Knight's *Rain In A Dry Land* is for you. It is a veritable twentieth century Acts of the Spirit and parts of the book partake of the dimensions of a Christian thriller. In fact, I can't remember when I have been as enthralled by such a wide range of Christian experience and insight, all within the compass of one story. Moreover, by virtue of the wide canvas on which John paints, the book has something for everyone, whether new minister or old hand; whether missionary, aspiring ordinand, Christian worker, ordinary layman; whether housewife, seeking teenager or young disciple.

John's thoroughly readable story nevertheless goes deep into what the Christian life is all about. Beyond that it succeeds remarkably in bringing together personal biography, spiritual quest, doctrinal reflection, ecclesiology, evangelism, healing, personal and congregational renewal, giving, stewardship, social concern, prophetic witness, family life, discipleship, missionary adventure plus glorious evidences of God's involvement in the affairs of man. It is all here – and more – in breathtaking range. And all written with compassion, humanity, lightness of touch, and humour.

However, what struck me most here was the extraordinary testimony to the faithfulness and living active power of God, our contemporary. If you doubt the miraculous this book will put an end to your doubts. Not only in his personal experiences of God's miraculous power, but in the mind-boggling evidences of God's supernatural workings and protection of His people in the 'Rhodesian' guerilla war, John brings us incontrovertible evidence of a God who is alive and well and on the job in our tattered twentieth century world.

What's more, the humble and honest quest described here for personal and congregational renewal, for preaching power, for counselling effectiveness and for pastoral relevance will particularly encourage every minister and pastor who knows dryness, or discouragement, or simply the desire to do better.

Personally, what challenged me most was John Knight's resolute determination to obey God whatever the cost, or risk, or consequence. And often for him and his family this was considerable.

This makes the book dangerous to pick up, because not only may it be the gentle tonic you need, it may also be spiritual dynamite to blast you into a new place in your discipleship.

The book is hugely enjoyable. But be warned. It may be more . . . !

And of course, if you also love Africa, as I do, that will be the cherry on the cake.

CONTENTS

AUTHOR'S NOTE

All Scripture references in the text (except where otherwise indicated) have been taken from the Good News Bible.

The present Zimbabwe has changed its name several times during this century. It was known as Southern Rhodesia when we entered it in 1936. From 1953–63 it amalgamated with Northern Rhodesia and Nyasaland to form The Federation of Rhodesia and Nyasaland. On the Dissolution of the Federation in 1963 – on the granting of Independence to Northern Rhodesia (renamed Zambia) and Nyasaland (renamed Malawi) – Southern Rhodesia became simply Rhodesia.

Just before the end of the guerilla war, which covered a little more than the 1970s – Prime Minister Ian Smith tried to accommodate black aspirations by stepping down as prime minister and appointing Bishop Abel Muzorewa in his place. He also sought to pacify both black and white groups by renaming the country Zimbabwe-Rhodesia. Neither action satisfied the Freedom Fighters. After the Lancaster House Agreement in 1979, Britain granted independence to the new ZIMBABWE in April, 1980, with Robert Mugabe of the Zimbabwe African National Union (Patriotic Front) as its first Prime Minister.

Shortly after Independence, a commission was established to review the names of cities, towns, villages, mountains, rivers, streets and so on. A number of names have been changed. In order to avoid confusion in the text, wherever a new name has been approved, that name has in most cases been used for the place throughout the history of this text.

The most commonly used names (with their original names given in parenthesis) are listed below:

CHIMANIMANI	(Melsetter)	KWE KWE	(Que Que)
CHIPINGE	(Chipinga)	MASVINGO	(Fort Victoria)
GWERU	(Gwelo)	MUTARE	(Umtali)
HARARE	(Salisbury)	NYANGA	(Inyanga)
KADOMA	(Gatooma)	NYAZURA	(Inyazura)

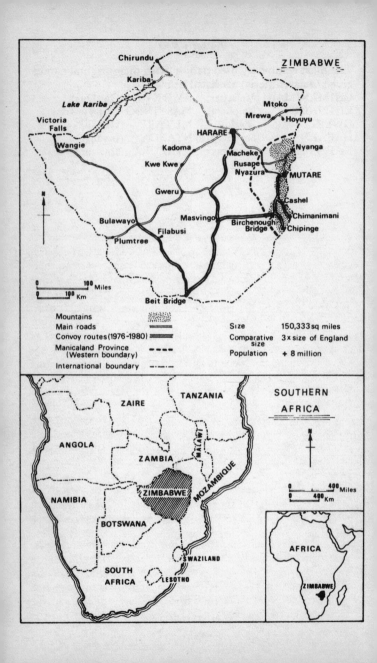

ZIMBABWE

Chirundu
Kariba
Lake Kariba
Victoria Falls
Wangie
Mtoko
Mrewa
Hoyuyu
HARARE
Kadoma
Macheke
Nyanga
Kwe Kwe
Rusape
Nyazura
MUTARE
Gweru
Cashel
Bulawayo
Masvingo
Birchenough Bridge
Chimanimani
Filabusi
Chipinge
Plumtree
Beit Bridge

0 ——— 100 Miles
0 ——— 100 Km

Mountains	Size	150,333 sq miles
Main roads	Comparative size	3 x size of England
Convoy routes (1976–1980)	Population	+ 8 million
Manicaland Province (Western boundary)		
International boundary		

SOUTHERN AFRICA

ZAIRE
TANZANIA
ANGOLA
ZAMBIA
MALAWI
MOZAMBIQUE
ZIMBABWE
NAMIBIA
BOTSWANA
SWAZILAND
SOUTH AFRICA
LESOTHO

0 ——— 400 Miles
0 ——— 400 Km

AFRICA
ZIMBABWE

ONE

DESECRATION OF GOD'S HOUSE

It was 7.20 a.m. on Sunday, 16 February, 1986. Many of us were in St John's Cathedral, Mutare (Zimbabwe), at the first of our Sunday morning Communion services. None of us had any knowledge of the stunning events that would follow two hours later. I had just read the Gospel for the day and was ready to preach. Yes, stranger than fiction perhaps, but at that moment I was led to change the theme I had earlier decided to preach on, and spoke instead on the subject of 'violence only begets more violence'. With hindsight, I believe God used that time to speak to me more than to anyone else. In addition, many listeners later drew comfort from this sermon when they received news of the desecration of the Cathedral.

In elaborating on the theme I pointed out that Scripture would have us carefully note: '"Vengence is mine", saith the Lord'. It was Jesus who gave us, His followers, a command that when anyone 'attacked' us, we were to turn the other cheek! I suggested that there was always such a temptation for us to want to defend 'our good name', and to want to hit back – verbally at least – against any who would lay false accusations against us, or against any who hurt us by word or deed.

I reminded them that Jesus was our most perfect example. Deserted by all His friends, He found Himself hanging on the Cross. Without any verbal expression of anger, or of the injustice of it all, He looked down on all those standing there mocking and jeering Him and said, 'Father, forgive them, for they know not what they do.' I pointed to the fact that the very first Christian martyr, Stephen, followed his master's example when he himself was being stoned to death. He commended his murderers to God with the words, 'Lord, lay not this sin to their charge.'

Those thoughts were still fresh in my mind when, two hours later, a vast mob stormed in and desecrated God's house during the next service. And because God had been so gracious in this way, we were ready with the right attitude of non-retaliation, and with a constant flow of prayer for forgiveness on the lips of all God's people kneeling there in the cathedral at the time. Perhaps the best way of describing the events surrounding that desecration, is to simply reproduce the report drawn up by myself as dean of the cathedral with the help of the Cathedral Council. We did this ten days after the event, after meticulously checking all the facts. The report reads as follows:

Tekere seizes $1¼ million of Church property: Police forbidden to intervene: Law and order non-existent in Mutare: Constitutional right to freedom of worship abrogated.

1. 8.50 a.m. 500-strong mob move on to St John's Cathedral property.
2. 8.55 a.m. Senior officer of Central Intelligence (CIO) warned leaders:
   (i) they had illegally invaded Church property,
   (ii) they were causing a disturbance of the peace and Church services were taking place, and
   (iii) he ordered them to leave the property.
3. 9.00 a.m. The mob ignored the CIO. He gave them fifteen minutes to leave, or else! (An empty threat as police previously ordered by officials not to intervene.)
4. 9.15 a.m. Church service commenced despite noise outside.
5. 9.20 a.m. Edgar Tekere (Chairman of Zimbabwe African National Union (Patriotic Front) ZANU (PF) Manicaland) entered the cathedral. He talked to Church leaders while the service was in progress. He was asked to stop the noise outside and invited to attend the service. Tekere said he had no wish to

listen, and that he was ordering his people to take possession of the property and drive us out.

6. 9.25 a.m. Tekere gave a brief speech to the demonstrators and, with the service still in progress, the mob poured into the cathedral, singing political songs, with many of them armed with sticks. The 500-strong mob:
   a) rocked and turned pews over to get the congregation out; many were forcibly manhandled and pushed outside;
   b) danced on the altar, beating out the candles with newspapers;
   c) knocked one priest over at the altar and dragged him down the full length of the cathedral flat on his back; another priest also manhandled out of the cathedral;
   d) children being led to safety thrown in all directions by the mob;
   e) one elderly lady, severely buffeted, carried out by parishioners in a state of shock.

7. 9.40–11.40 a.m. The dean, assistant priest and about twenty parishioners stayed to try and discover what the crowd wanted. No clear picture emerged except false stories told to squatters at St Augustine's Mission that the bishop wanted the land for his own (mythical) cattle.

8. 11.40 a.m. Mob started process of selecting two parishioners 'to be beaten until the bishop's whereabouts were revealed'. We walked through the mob and left as they fought over their choices.

9. Police refused to act. Several times the police were asked,
   i)   to remove the illegal mob from the church;
   ii) to protect parishioners;
   iii) to restore church property to the lawful owners.

The police explained that strict orders 'from above' ruled out ANY ACTION to protect lives and property, for this was 'Tekere business'. Tekere obviously above the law. Permission was also refused for us to enter the cathedral and lock up valuables, and permission refused us to switch off power to $60,000 pipe organ. (Serious damage possible as power may now have been on for nearly two weeks.)

10. 12.30 p.m. Assistant commissioner (police) advised the dean and his family to leave their home immediately as Tekere had given orders to invade their home. Although asked to do so, he regretted police were forbidden to intervene to protect individuals and property at the deanery in this 'Tekere matter'. Rule of law ceases?

11. 2.00 p.m. Two church members – the bishop's caretaker and another young man – caught by the mob in Main Street outside church offices. While being held by his thugs, Edgar Tekere personally brutally assaulted them in public. When they failed to give the information required, they were bundled into Tekere's car and driven off. Police in full view of the whole incident took no action to intervene. The young men were later hospitalised in Mutare General Hospital. Police not only did nothing to intervene but further, as witnesses, have apparently done nothing to lay charges of assault, battery and forcible abduction against Tekere.

12. 2.00 p.m. Mob rampages through assistant priest's garden throwing stones, banging on doors and windows demanding entry. Riot police removed the mob. (Not a designated house?)

13. 2.00 p.m. Mob took possession of bishop's house. (Ten days later we were still debarred from entry. On Thursday, 20 February, the SPCA inspector went to feed the dog, puppies and two flocks of chickens – unattended since Sunday. The mob forcibly evicted her and said the animals were to be left to starve to death or to die of thirst.)

Monday, 17 February to Wednesday, 26 February.

Daily, many have failed to gain entry to Church property. Many requests have been made to the police to intervene. They consistently refused because of 'orders from above'. Only three have gained access to the cathedral during this period – a lawyer who described the cathedral as being in 'a disgusting and filthy state', and a person who revealed himself to be a member of the British House of Lords (together with his wife) who insisted on entering the church to pray. One parishioner was assaulted on entering the church to pray – believing the mob had left – and laid charges at the police station. A message was relayed from police headquarters in Harare saying he had no right to enter his own cathedral without prior police permission.

On Tuesday, 25 February, the church re-possessed the parish office for four hours. The police refused to drive off the mob that tried to attack the offices. The mob leader said he had instructions from Tekere to break in the door if the staff did not get out, and threatened the women with rape. The staff left peaceably.

A PLEA. Every responsible citizen in Mutare is appalled at this outrage. The people are crying out to our government to come to our aid as a city and ensure that justice is seen to be done. Many policemen have told us of their horror at what is going on, and of the evil system of 'orders from above' that make them powerless to act. Some policemen who have wanted to help have been threatened with arrest if they do so. If those who perpetrate such lawless acts believe we are guilty of any crime, let them bring us to court, and let mob rule (when you can't get what you want legally) cease for ever in our beautiful new Zimbabwe.

As at midday, Friday, 28 February, the church had still not regained any of its properties. Report prepared by dean and Church Council of St John's Cathedral, Mutare, Zimbabwe. END OF STATEMENT.

A 'Stop Press' was added a few days later:

Police finally ordered to drive out those illegally holding our property late Saturday, early Sunday, 1–2 March, 1986. The dean and his family returned to their home on Sunday (2 March) – fifteen days after leaving with little more than what they stood up in. The bishop and his family hope to return soon. Thanks to thousands who supported St John's and the diocese with their love, prayer and messages. 'They' can take our property – but they can't stop the *living* Church. People will be heartened to know that all church services continued 'as usual' underground. Tuesday, 4 March: Mutare Ministers' Fraternal came out in total support of our cry for an end to the obvious breakdown of law and order, and the threat to freedom of worship in this country, and called on government to urgently remedy this situation.

The desecration of the cathedral, with the eviction of clergy and people from all church property for fifteen days, was staged to threaten the life of the bishop – or, at the very least, to intimidate him to such an extent that he would resign as bishop. Although the reason given for the invasion was the support of the leadership of a school in rebellion against the diocese, the main reason appeared to be a local political one. The principal character behind this was Edgar Tekere. He had been a cabinet minister in Robert Mugabe's first government after Independence was declared in April, 1980. Tekere was later charged with first-degree murder after he personally led a gang of his thugs, heavily armed with automatic weapons, against a farmer in the Goromonzi area near the capital. It was a commando-style affair with a farmer being chased across his farm, into his home, and gunned down in cold blood at point-blank range. The judge and his two assessors were unable to reach a unanimous verdict on the murder charge, but such was the revulsion in the country against such a cold-blooded and calculated murder, and at the blatant way Tekere took the law into his own hands to obtain what he could not get legally (the possession of the farm), Robert Mugabe removed him from the Cabinet.

It was not very long before the party in power appointed him to a powerful position as chairman of the party for the whole of the Manicaland Province, covering the eastern border area of the country. Soon afterwards he used a large threatening mob – in week-long demonstrations that closed down the civic centre – to bring about the enforced resignation of all the duly elected city councillors. As a consequence, the city was left in limbo without its executive arm until Tekere put forward his list of 'approved' candidates to be voted for several months later. This was the man who led the demonstrating thugs into the cathedral, ostensibly backing the cause of the rebellious school leadership he had befriended, but really for his own ends – to try and remove the bishop from his duly elected position. (Subsequently, in the presence of several witnesses, Edgar Tekere confessed his sorrow for his part in the invasion of the Cathedral and asked for God's forgiveness. We praise God for that. Early in 1987, the Prime Minister removed Tekere from his post as Manicaland Party Chairman in view of his past activities.)

In order to understand how we saw God's hands in preparing us for these days, and in discerning His protection over us, I need to go back in time.

TWO

EARLY DAYS

Though I have lived most of my life in Africa, I was actually born just inside England. That was at 'Hawk's Farm', near Penzance and Land's End, in 1936. I was born of staunch Anglican parents, with a strong tradition of Anglicanism running through the family.

After several trips 'down under' as a ship's surgeon, my father could not settle down to private practice in England after all the excitement of visiting places like India and Australia. Discovering that there was a need for doctors in Rhodesia, my father applied for a post in the Southern Rhodesia Medical Service. By the end of 1936, my parents and I were settled at Plumtree (western border) in the land of our choice, Southern Rhodesia. My brothers Keith (1937), Alan (1940) and Robert (1958) were all born in Rhodesia. Our extended family was small. My father left his parents behind in England, and his only brother Alan was a priest/headmaster of Adisadel College in the Gold Coast as it was then (Ghana). He and the students built the college themselves.

A year later, in 1937, Alan became the youngest bishop in the Anglican Communion when he was elected and consecrated as bishop of the diocese of British Guiana (now Guyana) in South America. Georgetown, the capital, is built on the marshes and his very beautiful cathedral was, at that time, the largest wooden cathedral in the world. It was, in recent years, beautifully restored. (Strangely enough, almost the first church we visited after returning to England recently is the oldest existing wooden church in the world – 856 AD –

at Greensted in Essex). Alan's parents joined him soon afterwards in British Guiana. Grandfather Knight, a retired headmaster, was Alan's secretary for many years; and Grandmother held sway as the mistress of Austin House (another very beautiful wooden building), the bishop's residence. Alan and my father were both great correspondents and never a week went past without them writing to each other. So we were kept fully informed on the state of the Church. We were aware that many of the priests were unmarried, and many posts unfilled, because of the shortage of finance. Despite the meagre resources that were available, one could only stand amazed at what was achieved in the development of the Church's work, especially in a vast country with virtually no roads (except around Georgetown). The courage and determination of those missionaries and local church workers was brought home by the hardships and difficulties that had to be faced, for example, by weeks of travel by canoe through areas like the Rupununi in the hinterland, and far from civilisation.

Guyana is an exceedingly hot and humid country where it is commonplace to have to shower and change one's clothes several times a day. Despite that, Alan was a stickler for dressing 'correctly', and wore full dress (frock coat and gaiters included) whatever the weather! Nor was he ever observed to sweat or perspire!

Alan, later Archbishop of the West Indies, remained a celibate all his life, strongly stressing – with a merry twinkle in those blue eyes of his – that he was married to the Church! To marry anyone else would be to commit bigamy! He died in Guyana in 1979, having served his diocese as bishop for forty-two years, and the Province of the West Indies as archbishop for twenty-nine years!

When we emigrated to Rhodesia, my mother left her own mother and two younger sisters in England. Granny Jess (a most wonderful woman to us as children, always full of fun and bubbling with excitement) and Aunt Joan both emigrated – separately – to Rhodesia after World War II. Joan, like my mother, was a trained state registered nurse. After a spell in a maternity unit, working for the government at the Lady Rodwell in Bulawayo, Joan devoted most of the next

thirty years of her life as a nurse to mission hospitals around
Rhodesia. This included her first station at St Patrick's,
Gweru. Here she was, for a long time, the only fully trained
member of staff and had to serve as administrator as well as
supervising the building of the new hospital. She seemed to
practically build the hospital single-handed, even to the
extent of driving in truck-loads of sand and stone in between
delivering babies in the maternity unit. She also worked at
Daramombe and St David's Hospital, Bonda.

What did appal me as a youngster was the absolute
pittance that Joan, and dedicated nurses like her, was given
by the missionary society and the diocese. People who not
only worked long hours (usually 'on-call' twenty-four hours a
day), but also had the responsibility for training new staff.
After giving up a life of comparative luxury in secular posts,
these mission employees were often expected to survive,
many miles from any shopping centre, in tiny, inadequately
equipped cottages on a nominal salary of about £25 a month.
Joan has since 'retired' to England and at seventy still works
full-time as matron of an old-people's home.

In addition, there were our 'own' priests, literally living
from hand to mouth because stipends were so abysmally low,
with housing and furnishing conditions often a cause for
much unhappiness to the families concerned. All these fac-
tors made a significant impact upon me during those impressionable teenage years.

Then there was the bigotry of the Church. My parents
were often ostracised and scorned because we had black
people come to stay with us in our house, both priests and
monks. People even walked out of the 'whites' church if one of
these black men took the service when our own rector was on
leave!

But there were also the good things about the Church.
Devoted priests and full-time workers – nuns, monks,
doctors, nurses, administrators – who gave of their all,
despite the often harsh conditions and seeming lack of care
and concern from the rest of the so-called Church 'militant'!
These people gave unstintingly of their love to us.

From my earliest memories life in the family revolved
around the church, the hospital and the home. At Christ-

mas, for instance, the day would start with attendance at a midnight service followed by singing in the choir or serving at the main service on Christmas morning. The rest of Christmas morning would then be spent at the hospital, giving out presents and Christmas cheer to patients and staff. Very often there would be a 'party' out in the hospital grounds for long-term patients such as those in TB (Tuberculosis) units.

This was particularly the case during the most impressionable years when we lived in Kadoma (Gatooma as it was known then, although as teenagers we had renamed it – long before the word gay came to have its present connotation – the 'Gay Tomb'.) At this period my father was the medical superintendent (or senior government medical officer as it used to be described) for Kadoma.

Only after the patients had been looked after would we start to think of our own Christmas celebrations with the opening of Christmas presents at afternoon tea, followed by Christmas dinner – with single doctors and nurses from the hospital being invited to celebrate with the family.

We were never allowed to miss a Sunday at church. We usually got involved as servers and in the choir. There were also the times of rebellion – but Dad always had the last say, and to church we went unless we could convince our own 'doctor in the house' that we really were sick. Even in the years when we lived at Filabusi (before moving to Kadoma in 1947) with no church or priest available. So Bishop Paget (later first archbishop of the newly created Province of Central Africa) agreed to the building of a lovely church, St Barbara-by-the-Spruit (stream), just outside our garden. It was built on the understanding that my father, a licensed lay reader (and later subdeacon) conduct Matins or Evensong on all Sundays when no 'trek' priest was available. For special festivals at Filabusi we would drive to Bulawayo. I still have vivid memories of the long drive on 'strip' roads (two parallel strips of tar, each about eighteen inches wide and far enough apart to fit the track of most vehicles, and very dangerous when passing or overtaking other vehicles) to Bulawayo on Christmas Eve to attend the midnight service. My youngest brother Alan would fall asleep on the kneelers at our feet. Then came the long drive home in the early hours of Christmas morning – with an exhausted Father Christmas tip-toeing in (presuming we were asleep) to deposit batches of toys in pillowcases at the foot of each bed at first light!

Something of the splendour of our Anglican heritage was brought home to us when we returned to England for the first time for a year's sabbatical which my father decided to take in 1948–49. We saw splendid churches and cathedrals, and the areas we stayed in seemed to have churches that were alive and packed with people. It was during that holiday, timed to coincide with my uncle's visit from British Guiana for the Lambeth Conference, that my two brothers and I were confirmed by my uncle in the old family church of St Jude-on-the-Hill in Hampstead, London. What a great occasion it was for the whole family! Unlike the first day of Pentecost, we did not see tongues of fire and neither did we hear a rushing mighty wind. Nor did we speak in tongues. But, as with so many people, we had been taught that 'those signs' were only for the new age when Christianity was brought to birth – and were no longer needed now.

So we were not taught to expect such things. What you don't expect, you don't ask for. But we were all well grounded in the doctrines of the Church, and taught the importance of a good prayer life, and the need for regular Bible study, and attendance at, and support of, the church.

Probably the closest I ever came, in those earlier days, to an understanding of the possibility of a *personal* involvement with Jesus, was through my mother. Regarded by many as a saint, to me she was one of the most loving, forgiving and caring people I have ever had the joy of knowing. She was the kind of woman who always looked for a person's good points and scarcely ever, to my knowledge, said an unkind thing about anyone – even against those who abused her and hurt her. I will never forget walking into the kitchen one Good Friday afternoon to find her sobbing her heart out. I was bowled over by the sight, threw my arms around her, and asked who it was that could have hurt her so. I shall never forget her reply, possibly because it was the last thing I expected at that moment. She had just returned from the 'Three Hour' Good Friday service. Using the most vivid imagery, she began to paint a picture of what Calvary meant to her. To her it was beyond belief that Jesus had allowed Himself to be crucified, willingly enduring the pain and suffering, the jeers and insults, in order to die on that Cross to pay the penalty for *her* sins. I found that hard to understand, taking into account the fact that Jesus died almost two thousand years before my mother lived. What *did* touch me deeply was the fact that my mother spoke of Jesus as someone who was as alive as I was – and that she loved Him as someone who lived and walked and talked with her! – and not of someone who lived immeasurably far away in heaven. It was a rare glimpse of what Jesus meant to her in her life. Although most devout and faithful in going to church and being involved in everything that was going on in the church (she was sacristan in many churches, making many sets of beautiful vestments and so on), the personal relationship she had with Jesus was something she rarely spoke about.

THREE

THE RELUCTANT PRIEST

My parents were determined that, whatever the cost to themselves, we three boys should have the best education possible. More to the point, they particularly wanted a school with a good Christian foundation. Through another family they were put in touch with a school that seemed to meet all their criteria – St John's College in Johannesburg, South Africa. It also appealed to my parents because for many years it was built up, with the quite magnificent stone buildings it now has, by the Community of the Resurrection from Mirfield, England. As a family we had many close links with this community through their work at St Augustine's Mission, Penhalonga, on the eastern borders of Rhodesia.

Although I had been living mainly at boarding schools since I was five, the very fact of being left at the age of eleven in a foreign country, two days and a night away by train from home, where family letters took a week to reach me, was probably one of the most traumatic experiences of my life. It took a long time, although I think I hid it well, for the heartache and the loneliness to wear off. Before too long a very full life at school helped me to adjust, along with a great determination to do well academically and with a great love for all manner of sporting activities abundantly catered for at the school. I knew what a tremendous financial sacrifice it was to my parents, even to the extent of my parents continuing to maintain their 1937 vintage car during most of my nine years at St John's! For brief periods, when my two brothers joined me, the cost was crippling. However, Keith left after a couple of years to transfer to a technical school, and Alan returned to a Rhodesian school because he twice picked up a virus that partially, and temporarily, paralysed him.

'Church' played a significant part in the life of the school. Not that many seemed to take their faith very seriously, but compulsory morning and evening worship every Sunday and daily prayers during the week in the school chapel proved a real bore to many. Some alleviated their boredom by serving at the altar, and the one position aimed for by most was that of thurifer with the chance (rather like a drum-major with his mace) of executing a number of adventurous movements, including 360 degree swings with a thurible full of red hot coals and incense. To be a thurifer, as a senior boy in the school, carried status! I endured much of my time in the chapel because I found pleasure singing in the choir (as treble, then alto, and finally as a bass). The choir, especially through its musical productions, enjoyed considerable prestige in Johannesburg's music circles.

Even during those times when I was serious about my relationship with God, I was often filled with a sense of failure. There were the problems of continuing sin, the failure to pray and read the Bible regularly, and the failure to worship God with any sense of reality. There was, moreover, a growing belief within me that I would never succeed in my efforts to be good enough to enter heaven. It is strange perhaps, but of all the many sermons I had to listen to in the school chapel, the one and only statement I remember to this day was a brief comment thrown out by a visiting preacher. He simply mentioned the fact that it had been a grievous shock to him to discover that in its fifty-five-year existence (nearly forty of them run by a community of monks), the number of priests produced by this school could be counted on the fingers of one hand! Within three years that number was almost to double!

But I did not really believe that that concerned *me* at the time. As the eldest child my dream had always been to follow in my father's footsteps. Whenever opportunity offered during schools holidays I would be found in the hospital with my father, both in the wards and in theatre. I not only loved the life, but was greatly excited by all that the future held for me.

And everything on the horizon looked wonderful – until the beginning of my last term at school. Soon my final examinations would be over, and it was anticipated that I would enter medical school in Capetown the following year.

It is difficult to convey the shock that followed. As often happened in a school like ours in the run-up to major examinations, many of us got up early on a weekday morning to attend the voluntary Communion services. We hoped that God would give us extra help for doing these extra stints! It was in a quiet moment on one of these mornings when I found myself looking up at the altar, probably with no other thought than that the breakfast bell had just gone and it wouldn't be more than a moment now before we got out of chapel. The priest was standing there, about to give the blessing, with arms and hands lifted high, and head pointed 'heavenwards'. In the moment of silence that followed I was conscious of what seemed to be a voice saying to me: 'This is what I would have you do, my son.' The first thing I remember feeling was an embarrassment that others had been disturbed by this shattering of the silence (and of course they heard nothing); and then, only secondly, came the shock that such a suggestion could be put to me! Not only because it was so totally contrary to the dreams and longings of my heart for the future, but even more so because I did not believe I was the kind of person God could, or would, use.

A few days later I found I just had to share this with someone. I went to see Nobby Clarke – a giant of a man who had been priest and headmaster of St John's for twenty years and was on the point of retiring. I had always found it difficult to think of him as a priest, and thought he at least would tell me not to take this suggestion seriously. But I discovered new depths in him that day, and a gentleness and kindness that I did not think he had. Strangely, he understood the turmoil boiling within me. He understood my love of medicine and desire to help people who were sick. He put his finger on the fact that I could look forward to a life of relative affluence and greater acceptability in the community, and he understood my horror of a life of hardship, poverty and ridicule – a view that had built up over my close contact with many priests over the years. It was almost as if he could read my mind. But he never tried to influence me in either direction. All he said was that if this was a call from God, I could not ignore it. Rather than make a quick decision, he advised me to come back to school for an extra year. And even there he solved my problem about the added expense for my father which immediately came to mind. Before I could say a word, he told me not to worry about this aspect, as he would arrange with the governors of the school for me to be given a scholarship covering all tuition and boarding costs for the next year. It was a most generous gift, and the following year was spent much more on the 'arts' side, taking up extra subjects such as Greek, and with time to wait on God.

Although I received no further clear 'directions' from God, it became clearer and clearer to me during that year that the original 'call' could only have come from God. It was most certainly not anything that I would have wished for, so there could only be one source for that command. Not that the knowledge made it any easier for me to say 'yes' to the call. Not only did I feel totally unworthy and unacceptable as a person, but I knew so little, theologically speaking, that there was no way I could put up a reasonable argument for the existence of God or for the defence of the faith 'once delivered to the saints!'

So it was, at the end of that year, almost literally with my heart in my mouth, that I said 'YES'. My only request to my father was that I should do my training overseas. My request was granted and there followed three years at Leeds University, and a final two years at Theological College, where I completed the General Ordination Examination of the Church of England. Having satisfied the examiners, and earned enough money as a Rolls-Royce chauffeur to refurbish my wardrobe and meet some of the expenses of my return, I sailed home to Rhodesia. Naturally, there was great excitement at my return, but overshadowing it all was my own feeling of total inadequacy, and a fear within me that I would be unable to cope with the burdens and tasks of ministry. I was still utterly fearful of speaking up in a group of people – let alone holding forth in a pulpit. And I felt incapable of carrying on a theological argument; the only way I could was to retire to my books and write a reply! How then could God take this material – John Knight – poor and ineffective as it was, to preach the Good News powerfully and effectively? All I knew was that I was rather like a robot being moved on from one stage to another, and soon enough someone was going to discover that I was in the wrong job.

A few years previously the original Diocese of Southern Rhodesia had been divided into two dioceses – Mashonaland and Matabeleland. My selection for ministry training had come from the poorer of the two dioceses, Matabeleland. Its first bishop was a long-standing friend of the family, James Hughes. He had been dean of Georgetown Cathedral in British Guiana under my uncle, prior to becoming a bishop in the West Indies. On the creation of the See of Matabeleland, he was chosen as its first bishop and 'translated' from the West Indies. He it was who ordained me deacon in the Cathedral of St John the Baptist, Bulawayo, in September 1961 and appointed me to serve my diaconate in St Cuthbert's Gweru (Gwelo) under the care of another long-standing friend of the family, Canon Reg Adams. A more faithful pastor and servant of God I could not have wished for as my first mentor.

But 'bigamy' had begun to rear its ugly head. A few years earlier, Grandmother Knight left British Guiana on the death of her husband and came to live with us. She was imbued with her Bishop Alan's principles, and she was delighted to come to Rhodesia and have an old friend, James Hughes, as her bishop. James had also been a celibate for most of his life. Then came the shock. Reports came back that James, who was supposed to be attending Lambeth Conference in England, was frequently absent from debates. It was later discovered that he was courting – and came back to Rhodesia with a wife! Grandmother was so shocked that she took to her bed for a week, and wouldn't speak to anyone. It was a long time before she could begin to accept the *fait accompli* and welcome James and his wife back into our house with good grace! Not long after, Reg Adams – also in his sixties – had up and married Molly Coppock! Both men had been confirmed bachelors! So when I came to announce my own nuptials two years later, Grandma was resigned to the fact of declining standards! But before speaking of that, I need to speak of my first two years in Gweru.

FOUR

THE FIRST FALTERING STEPS

My arrival in Gweru in 1961 to serve my diaconate was not, to my mind, an auspicious one. The Church Council informed me that they had secured a room for me at a local hotel. Although very close to the church, I soon discovered it to be the 'red light' hotel of the area. The rooms were anything but clean and my first night there was a nightmare. I woke an hour after falling asleep to find myself riddled with bites from head to foot. Bed bugs! With nothing to treat them with, I found the only way to bring relief was to spend the night in the bath. Although the bed bugs were adequately dealt with, the constant comings and goings in the rooms around me were not conducive to rest and study. I appealed to the Council to find me a small flat or house. They regretted that the parish was finding it hard enough to pay the diocesan assessment to meet the stipend of the rector – let alone the extra assessment for a deacon they had not asked for and couldn't really afford! Finally they relented to the extent that they gave me permission to find somewhere else to live. The condition laid down was that it was not to cost more than £17 a month, the amount they were paying for my furnished room at the hotel!

I managed to find a semi-detached house of sorts. It had a bedroom with no windows, so the bedroom door had to stay open to provide air. A small sitting room completed the main part of the house. The kitchen, bathroom and toilet had been made possible by converting a small lean-to porch. The outside wall of this 'porch' had no windows, but was covered with mosquito gauze – lovely in summer but decidedly cold in winter. I thought the landlord had been particularly generous to this impecunious clergyman when he offered to leave a large double wardrobe in the bedroom for my use. It was only later when I came to give the room a good clean that I discovered that its real function was to cover a large 3ft × 1ft hole in the floor! The old second-hand furniture provided by the parish made it a little difficult to entertain. This included a bed and mattress, one occasional chair, one dining-type chair, one table for dining purposes with a 24" × 30" top, and a small rug. Most of my social life therefore took place in the kitchen, where we could use the stove top and sink for additional seats!

Eighteen months later I was able to rent, still for the same amount, a tiny 'prefabricated' house that was without any insulation whatsoever, so it was very hot in summer and exceedingly cold in winter – but more about that later.

My early ministry got off to a shaky start. At theological college we literally received no training in what to do and say when visiting people in the parish. Nor were we equipped or prepared to deal with awkward customers, or with people who were chronically ill and dying. I got quite good at drinking tea, talking about the weather, and then the family, and then politics, and back to weather and sport. How to talk about Jesus, or even to get on to the subject – that was the problem. No one had taught me how to do that, or taken me with them (like a master teaching his disciple) and shown me how it was done. And what do you say to the dying apart from comforting them by saying 'Cheer up! You are going to be fine' when you know jolly well they need to prepare themselves for death? And what about the mentally ill? During my two years at theological college we only once visited a hospital – for an hour's visit – no other institution was ever visited! Each one of us was given a bed to visit, and mine turned out to be occupied by someone who had gone round the bend! But no instruction was given on what to do or say. In this first parish there were some homes that were so notoriously difficult that I would drive around the block half a dozen times just to gather up enough courage to go in. And even then I sometimes 'chickened out'! Of course there were

also the more humorous moments. On one occasion I
knocked on the door of a house and a very small child opened
the door. She took one look at me and fled back down the
passage shouting, 'Mummy, Mummy, God's come!' That
was her understanding of the person that she had seen
standing in the pulpit the day before.

As a deacon in one's first year of ministry, there are
limitations on what one can do (or, should I say, could do?).
Amongst other things I couldn't celebrate at a Communion
service (although a 1987 report in the Church of England
newspaper on a meeting of the Anglican Evangelical Alliance
indicates pressure from one part of the Church for that to be
changed). Nor was I allowed, in the eyes of the Church, to
perform marriages because I could not 'bless' the couple.
Only a priest could do that! (A quarter of a century later the
Church of England is in the process of changing all that, too.
It is doing this so that the new permanent order of female
deacons can perform marriages. The Bishop of St Germans
is quoted as saying: '"The whole thing hinges on the question of 'Can a deacon bless?' The rule of thumb Catholic view
would be that the functions of absolution, presiding at the
Eucharist, and blessing are preserved for priests." But the
argument was advanced that blessings are in fact a form of
prayer. In the original Latin, they employ the subjunctive to
enjoin God to do something. And prayer may – and should –
be practised by anyone. So deacons may bless and solemnise
a marriage' (Andrew Brown in *The Independent* 5/11/86).

In 1961 I could do neither. Although the Church did not
allow me to perform marriages, I was – in the eyes of the state
– licensed to perform marriages as a legal marriage officer! I
had only been in the parish a few months when Reg went on
leave. He had arranged that a school chaplain from Guinea
Fowl – a Welshman – would come in and take all the
Communion services. Reg also asked him to conduct a
wedding that had already been booked. I was left in charge
of everything else. On the day before the wedding, a
Friday, the stand-in priest had taken a service in the
church. As the service ended, I reminded him about the
wedding for the next day. He replied rather petulantly,
'Of course I've remembered it!' He then went across to the

parish office and our very efficient parish secretary also
asked if he had remembered the wedding. She was very upset
afterwards because he apparently 'flew off the handle'
at her for implying that he was likely to forget such an
appointment!

Saturday was my day off and, as usual, I went to visit
friends in Kwe Kwe about forty miles away. But because we
had someone dying in hospital, I decided to cut my day short
and come back and visit the old lady. It was a good thing I
did. After visiting her, I came back to the parish office to
spend the rest of the day continuing my search through the
archives for material for the history of the Church in Gweru
that I was writing. Subconsciously I was aware of people
arriving for the wedding, and then noted the usual lull as the
guests awaited the bride. I heard her car draw up, watched
her move into the church and heard the organist break into
the wedding march. Thinking all was well, I went on with my
work. It was quite a surprise to find a harassed man knocking
at the office door a few minutes later. When I opened it, (he
had no knowledge of who I was as I was wearing shorts and a
bright tartan shirt) he asked where he could find the priest.
Apparently the bride had arrived alongside the groom before
it began to dawn on the congregation that there was no priest
– and the bride was taken into the vestry in floods of tears. I
telephoned the priest's house out at Guinea Fowl, but there
was no answer and I presumed that he had broken down on
the way in. I realised I could have a problem on my hands if
he was not found. Fortunately the bride had worked for the
telephone exchange. I needed to get hold of the bishop's
deputy, the bishop being away overseas, to get permission to
conduct the wedding if necessary. He lived a hundred miles
away in Bulawayo. I gave the girls at the exchange his name
and home number, explained to the girls their friend's
problem, and said they had to find Canon Pugh wherever he
was, and get permission for me to take the wedding. Mean-
while I jumped into my little Fiat 600 and roared out to
Guinea Fowl, ten miles away. The priest was not to be found.
On my way back into town I picked up my cassock from the
house and covered my sporting gear with it. On arriving back
at the church I heard that permission had been granted for

me to officiate on the understanding that the couple's wedding would be 'blessed' by a priest when the rector returned from leave.

Now came the most agonising part for me. I had never taken a wedding before – or been shown what to do. (My responsibility for conducting weddings lay many months in the future, so I had not thought there was any urgency to prepare for that!) I had to take the service with pauses between each prayer, so that I could read the rubrics in order to discover what I had to do next. We got through it in the end. The father of the bride was flaming mad and said he would never darken the doors of the church again (we certainly hadn't seen anything of him before), and the priest concerned tried to tell Reg that I had failed to remind him about it. Fortunately my parish secretary was able to support me – even if Reg doubted my word, which he didn't.

That was not the end of the story. About ten years later I was attending a reunion of pupils from one of the Gweru schools. I just could not take my eyes off one young couple. I knew that I knew them – but I couldn't 'place' them. At the end of the evening they came up to me and said that I obviously couldn't remember who they were! I agreed! They then told me with great glee that they were the first couple I had ever married, and far from carrying sad memories of the seeming calamities of the day, had had a great time dining-out on the story ever since – even to the extent of relating that I had dressed in such a hurry that it was obvious that I did not have a clerical collar on, for a fair bit of my tartan collar was sticking out instead!

Not surprisingly, my preaching was pathetic, but then I had always been terrified of any kind of public speaking. At theological college we had a mere two opportunities to preach the Gospel during our two-year course – both in local village churches, in front of tutors and fellow students. It was a devastating experience. When it came to my second time round, my principal tried to encourage me by saying that my content had been good, but . . . His advice on what to do about it? Go and preach into a tape recorder – and then listen to yourself! Yes, I fell asleep! That was the sum total of my practical instruction in preparing me to be a preacher of the

Word. Fortunately in this first parish I had a most devoted
Christian, Pam Braatvedt, wife of the breweries manager to
help me! A speech and drama expert, she took me in hand for
over a year, underlining the parts of my sermon that should
be highlighted, and encouraging me to practise preaching it
until some life was brought into the words. Just before they
were transferred from Gweru, Pam told me I would never
really get anywhere until I threw away my written sermons
(written word for word, because I didn't dare take my eyes off
the paper!) There was no way that I was going to do that, and
it was many years before I took that plunge.

Also in 1961, first year of my diaconate, the great dream of
bringing the whole of Central Africa together – which had
seemed to be a dream fulfilled when the Federation of
Rhodesia and Nyasaland was created in 1953, but which was
to collapse like a pack of cards in 1963 – was now crumbling
around our ears. Hastings Banda and Kenneth Kaunda were
rising to power, and their ascendance brought with it an
economic slump that bankrupted many businesses, and a
rise in the number of those emigrating. St Cuthbert's suffered
a great deal during those days, but it did also, fortuitously,
benefit tremendously from the changes which were instituted
at the time. As I arrived in the parish it was decided to sell the
hall, rectory and church (too small for the congregation) and
build a grand new complex on an 'island' site that would
make St Cuthbert's a real focal point in the town. Because of
the slump, the tenders for the building were ridiculously low
– building firms being only concerned with keeping their
work forces together to ride out the economic slump. We
built a magnificent new church to seat over 300, a church
hall, a well-equipped kitchen and store rooms, together with
another large hall that housed the parish office, priest's
vestry and three other rooms that doubled as choir vestries
and Sunday School classrooms. All this was built on a large
'box' plan with interconnecting covered ways. The total cost
of all this was an unbelievably low figure of £40,000 and
during my five years in Gwelo we paid off nearly three-
quarters of that debt. Yes, people would give for a building,
but it was almost impossible to obtain money to pay for
ministry! That church has now become a very fitting

Cathedral Church for the new Diocese of the Lundi when it was created in July, 1981.

Many fund-raising efforts were undertaken to help pay off the mortgage on the church as quickly as possible. In the most successful fête, over £2,500 profit was made over one afternoon and evening. As the evening drew to a close, we decided that it would not be wise to leave the money in the church safe over the long weekend, Monday being a Bank Holiday. After most people had gone home, we had a quick meeting to decide where to put the money. Finally one of my fellow organisers offered his cold rooms as a perfectly secure place. At the time we did not foresee the consequences of our decision. First of all we had failed to tell the rector about what we had done, so when he came down to open the safe on Tuesday morning he was stunned to find it empty. The second consequence involved the bank. Because of the weekend cold-room treatment, all the coins had a tendency to stick together, and were very cold. We were not popular – and it took some time before those girls at the bank were able to look back and laugh at the incident!

The new church also had its drawbacks. It was almost impossible to hear most speakers because of the tremendous echo in the building as a result of the massive concrete pillars, ceiling and floors, and the plastered brick and concrete surfaces of all the walls. We couldn't afford carpeting – apart from the centre aisle. We had a great time searching Bulawayo, a hundred miles away, for materials that would match the paintwork of the walls and having curtains made that covered the side walls 'curtain-style'. That helped to absorb some of the echo. (Acoustic tiles were almost unobtainable, cost a great deal, and absorbed or attracted dust – and repainting would mean the loss of their acoustic properties). The final effort at solving the problem was the purchase of heavy material made up like a rich, heavy curtain to completely drape the whole of the west wall. It was an enormous job to have all that footage made up in a small upholstery business in Gweru. It was then erected, using scaffolding, to hang almost from the apex of the roof, and drawn back with special ties in order to fall free of, and down the sides of, the great west doors. All these things helped a little. But we

discovered that the best solution to acoustic problems was a
packed church – for all the clothes acted as an absorbent
material! That was proved in quick succession at the dedication service, my ordination to the priesthood, and my
marriage.

Exactly a year after my ordination as a deacon I was
ordained to the priesthood on 29 September, 1962. The
ordination was taken by Kenneth Skelton who had just been
consecrated as the new bishop of Matabeleland, in succession to Archbishop James Hughes. (Bishop Skelton recently
retired as Bishop of Lichfield.)

It was about this time that I had become very much aware
of a young teacher in the Sunday School, Jill Bradbury. By
mid-January we were, to the delight of our families and the
parish, engaged to be married, but there were problems
about the cost of a wedding, and suitable housing. Jill's
mother was a widow and still struggling to bring up a family,
and there was no way that she could afford to provide a
reception. This was a problem because, between us, we – Jill
a local girl, and myself as local priest – knew many of the
people in Gweru, all of whom would expect to be invited. We
had virtually decided that the only solution was to go
elsewhere and have a quiet wedding. However many of the
ladies in the two women's groups would not have this, and
offered to provide a reception as their own special gift to us.
Old family friends of Jill's from out of town – specialists in
floral decorations – provided banks of flowers in the church
and for the reception. All in all, over six hundred people were
catered for, and we have never failed to bless and thank them
all for their love and generosity.

The wedding day itself, Saturday, 31 August, 1963, was
everything one could wish for – dawning bright and clear and
remaining sunny and warm all day. A choir forty-strong had
spent hours rehearsing special music for the occasion; at the
end of the service they presented us with a taped recording of
the whole service – done without our being aware of it. Even
Jill's promise to obey came over loud and clear, and recorded
for all time! It was a morning wedding, with the church
packed to the doors and overflowing outside. Reg Adams, as
rector and as long-standing friend of the family, conducted

the marriage ceremony and preached the sermon. Bishop
Skelton celebrated the sung Eucharist that followed. The
wonderful luncheon reception took place in the church
grounds. Altogether a most wonderful and memorable event.

Unfortunately our housing problem was still not resolved.
The tiny 'prefabricated' house that I had recently obtained
(within the £17 limit the Church Council still insisted on)
would, I hoped, be an improvement for my new bride –
certainly better than a house with a windowless bedroom.
However, my parents stayed in the house while Jill and I
were away on our honeymoon, and decided it was so un-
healthy to live in that they rented another house for us. Until
the parish was fortunate enough to have another house
bequeathed to them about eighteen months later, my parents
paid the additional rent that was needed.

We did indeed have a very difficult Church Council to deal
with, even though many of the people on it *were* constructive
and helpful, and some were numbered amongst our dearest
friends. They, too, agonised with us at many of the decisions
that were made. There was one particular group that looked
upon every meeting as an opportunity to be as 'cussed' as
they could – and appeared to take delight in being that way
inclined. My rector was a very sick man towards the end, and
I believe that their attitude – their constant threats to resign
over almost every issue if they did not get their way – broke
his heart and hastened him into a premature grave. Of the
next two rectors after I left, the first also died in office, and the
second had a heart attack that invalided him out of the
parish. The Gweru parish was known to be notoriously
difficult. As with so many parishes it suffered from an acute
shortage of money, literally living from one crisis to the next,
with an everlasting stream of jumble sales, fêtes and other
money-raising efforts to try to make ends meet. It was
difficult not to feel like a beggar continually trying to wheedle
some more money out of pockets that seemed to be permanently zipped up. Not surprisingly, many complained
that the church was always asking for money.

Like so many other Christians at that time – ministers
more particularly perhaps – I found close contact with
members of other Churches quite a problem. Efforts were

being made, through Ministers' Fraternals, to get the leaders
of Churches together, but very often if the minister of one
Church attended, then another wouldn't. With my upbringing, only Anglicans were considered to be members of the
true Church. Some of the other Churches (Roman Catholics,
Methodists, Presbyterians, Baptists – for example) were all
right, but . . .! But Pentecostals were categorised by me – as
well as by most of the Churches I have mentioned – as
outside the true Church completely. 'They' were people – I
had always been told – who actually went beserk during their
services. I was so intrigued – and yet so frightened of being
contaminated by their mumbo-jumbo – that one dark night I
crept up to the window of one of their churches to have a look
in. I was disappointed! Nevertheless I still kept my distance,
particularly when I discovered the feeling was mutual, and
most of 'them' wouldn't come to the Fraternal meetings
because they regarded all of us as unsaved!

Members of the Fraternal did help me over one issue with
my rector. He was one of the old guard who insisted that the
clergy should be dressed in dark suits (or flannels and jackets
of sombre hue), a black shirt, and dog collar! One day I
turned up at our parish office wearing a safari suit composed
of a pair of shorts and matching short-sleeved jacket in a light
cool material – ideal for the tropics. Reg was visibly upset
and told me it was totally unbecoming attire for a priest. I
have a persistent streak in me and wore it to the monthly
Fraternal meeting that afternoon, where the suit was greeted
with delight. A few days later several other city pastors were
sporting the new fashion. Reg resigned himself to the fact and
just accepted that I was different. At least I still wore the
regulation black shirt and dog collar. Those, too, also disappeared years later.

One attitude that arose in that Ministers' Fraternal did
cause me deep anger for many years. Quite a number of those
men had the effrontery (in my eyes) to assert that they were
sure they were going to heaven! The sheer arrogance of their
stance – apparently believing themselves to be holy enough
to go to heaven – made my blood boil. Only years later was I
brought to an understanding of what Scripture said about
this. It was to change my life.

What a far cry so much of this seemed to be from the kind of victorious Church one reads about in the New Testament – a Church that grew by leaps and bounds, was filled with enthusiasm, had a sense of purpose, and was assured of God's provision for all its needs:

> Peter made his appeal to them and with many other words he urged them, saying, 'Save yourselves from the punishment coming on this wicked people!' Many of them believed his message and were baptised, and about three thousand people were added to the group that day. They spent their time in learning from the apostles, taking part in the fellowship, and sharing in the fellowship meals and the prayers. Many miracles and wonders were being done through the apostles, and everyone was filled with awe. All the believers continued together in close fellowship and shared their belongings . . . (Acts 2:40–44).

There was little evidence of this in my ministry or in the ministry of the Church of the 1960s. Despite the fact that some well-known theologians of that time did not believe in miracles, I felt that there was something missing. However, more than anything else I began to feel not only inadequate as a priest, but a real all-round failure. After visiting a person who was chronically ill and praying for him with no apparent result, the subsequent visits became more and more difficult for me because there was nothing I could do or say to help that person. We had written miracles out of normal Christian experience. So what was left?

There were also moments in our times of worship that gave me cause for concern. Would we rattle through the prayers – as we so often did – if Jesus was actually present there? Is that the way we would speak to Him? Of course we wouldn't. But we did! One priest known to me – and there were, and are, others like him – took pride in the fact that he could get through the whole of the Communion Liturgy in seventeen minutes flat on a weekday morning! It had no more meaning than listening to a machine gun set on automatic and rapid fire. The noise was there, but there was no hope of distinguishing between the individual shots. For all too many of us, the practice of our religion had become as impersonal as that.

Reg Adams died in 1965, and I was left as acting rector of the parish. It was a traumatic year in many ways. Ian Smith, Prime Minister of Rhodesia, – together with his full Cabinet – unilaterally declared Rhodesia independent of Britain (UDI – 11 November, 1965). For a short time, especially as it was advocated by the then Archbishop of Canterbury, we anxiously wondered if a British Task Force would fly in to try and wrest back control from the Rhodesian Front Party. Would it be a repeat of the American War of Independence (so similar in many ways) all over again? Ministry-wise I seemed to spend a disproportionately large part of my time getting back into church those people who took exception – at one time or another – to the archbishop's, or other bishops', statements on the political issues of our day. From the ministry point of view, by the beginning of 1966 I had had enough, and felt that the only solution left open to me was to leave.

We did have one final blessing before leaving Gweru: the miracle birth of our son Andrew in December, 1965. Was it indeed a miracle, and God's way of trying to show us that miracles still do indeed happen? Jill had been in the maternity home in Harare for some weeks with severe toxaemia before it was suddenly discovered that there was no longer a foetal heartbeat. Partly because my father was in the medical profession, there were several specialists in the theatre when Andrew was born. We were told later that Andrew held the record for the length of time after birth without breathing – and yet surviving. After trying everything possible, they finally injected something directly into the brain – and he started to breathe. He had a large lump there on the top of his head for nearly a year! Even that was not the end of the story. He was able to survive the next few weeks because of a special incubator which had recently arrived from the United States. It was the gift of a wealthy Harare business family who had themselves lost a child because there was no machine of this kind in Rhodesia. Their generosity made it possible for our son Andrew to be the first child to be saved in this unit. He has gone from strength to strength from that day on.

Despite the joy and wonder of our own son, I knew that I could not continue any longer in Gweru. Was it also time to look for some other kind of work?

FIVE

SIDE-STEPPING INTO BUSINESS

With hindsight, I am sure that the main reason for my unhappiness and disillusionment in the ministry was that I was continually trying to minister in my own strength. But God, in His wonderful way, placed another person in my path who was able to help me along and rekindle within me a hope for the future. He was another friend of the family, Cecil Alderson. Cecil had been a bishop in a number of dioceses in South Africa, and had only recently been appointed bishop of the neighbouring Diocese of Mashonaland. After hearing my side of the story, he suggested that it was time for me to make a change from my parish in Gweru. He offered me the tiny parish of St Mark's, Ruwa, which had probably one of the most beautiful churches in the country, and covered the small farming areas of Bromley, Ruwa and Melfort just to the east of Harare (Salisbury). The bishop soon revealed that the parish was only somewhere for me to 'park' myself, even though it soon grew to an area of over 10,000 square miles with chapelries (Arcturus, Mrewa, Hoyuyu, Mtoko) extending to the eastern border of Zimbabwe on the main road to Malawi, and a central mission station. The mission (so termed because it was not considered to have achieved the maturity of parish status) had a central church, junior and senior schools and the Shearly Cripps Children's Home, together with eight churches and schools on outlying stations. In addition to everything else, the priest-in-charge of a mission station was also manager of the schools. The real purpose behind placing me at Ruwa was to make use of one of my natural gifts for the benefit of the Church. Accountancy being my special hobby, Bishop Cecil asked me to conduct audit checks on many of the missions of the diocese.

As I undertook that task, I discovered that the missions and their school systems – where priests acted as managers for anything from fifteen to thirty schools – were in a terrible financial mess. Not only that, but many of the things that came to light as a result of my enquiries literally broke the heart of Bishop Cecil. He died very suddenly on a brief visit to South Africa soon afterwards.

It was my unhappy duty to welcome our new bishop, Paul Burrough from England, with an alarming picture of gross mismanagement throughout much of our school and mission system, with many people 'on the make'. The sheaf of reports would have been enough to break the back, or the heart, of most men before they even got started. Fortunately, and perhaps as a result of his incarceration in a Japanese prisoner of war camp for most of the Second World War, the new bishop was made of sterner stuff. One of his feats in the early days of his episcopacy was to walk 400 miles through the African bush during the forty days of Lent to meet the people!, a walk which included crossing rivers in flood. And he walked the legs off anyone who cared to join him for short stretches!

Soon after Bishop Paul's arrival, I was due to undertake an audit of yet another mission. I had sent a letter to the priest, advising him that he would be required to prepare all the various record books, that I would want to see, for a given date. The bishop was horrified to receive a letter from the priest threatening my life if I set foot in his mission. Being very new, all the bishop could think to do was to call on the archdeacon, David Neaum, who was to accompany me that day, and ask David to take the bishop's episcopal ring as a mark of the bishop's authority for the visit. David just laughed, handed the ring back to the bishop, and said: 'You don't have to worry about John. He carries a revolver under the seat of his car!' The priest was not there when we arrived, and so we had to ask his wife to unlock the office for us so that we could start our checks. The priest arrived back late in the afternoon very much under the weather. After explaining to him that he would never get out of the mess he was in until he accepted help and advice, we finally got his co-operation for the rest of the week that we were there. Another priest was so antagonistic that he removed all the books from his office and consistently refused to let us have sight of them. The bishop eventually had to write and tell him that unless everything that was needed was brought to the bishop's office by Easter Sunday, he would be permanently removed from the ministry.

On another occasion I received a note from the bishop informing me that a certain mission was complaining that the previous priest-in-charge had taken the mission typewriter and duplicator away with him – would I please check it out. I went to see the priest and found a typewriter and duplicator in his office. On being questioned about them, he said that they were his own property, so I asked how he had bought them. He then explained that when he went to Mission 'X', they had neither of these essential pieces of office equipment. So with great personal initiative, he had purchased them. On being asked where the money came from, he finally agreed that he had paid for them with mission cheques, but argued that it was his 'initiative' that had made their acquisition possible. Knowing that he didn't have a car in his latest job, I said to him: 'If, with great initiative, you save up mission money here and finally go out and buy a car for yourself to use on this job, will it be yours when you move on to another mission?' 'Oh, no Father! That is a big thing!' was the reply. One by one I loaded the typewriter and duplicator into my car and drove off.

It is important to stress that much of the blame for the financial mismanagement in the missions and schools was due to lack of training and supervision from the top. Of course it will be argued that black priests raised such a song and dance about not being given responsibility to run the missions without white overall leadership that the Church moved *too* rapidly and handed over total control to priests who, by and large, were given no instruction on how to keep accounts or on how to manage their financial affairs. The result was a total disaster. Furthermore, to compound the problem, the Church had 'required' that regular financial returns be submitted to head office. When these did come in they were stacked away but never checked – so that the priest, who was at least trying, never had his mistakes picked up and corrected. Those who never sent in any returns were never chased up. Bishop Alderson realised this, and for this reason asked me to undertake this job and try to unravel the mess that had accumulated over the previous ten to fifteen years.

We did have one priest who really did things in style. He lived far from 'civilisation', and as I found it difficult to carry out an audit while accepting the hospitality of the person one is auditing – they can usually ill afford it – I decided to take a caravan. David Neaum accompanied me on this trip. On our first day there the priest insisted we have lunch with him. It was magnificent. Roast beef and Yorkshire pudding – with rosella jelly and all the trimmings. The second day it was roast duck with all that you would expect a high class hotel to serve as an accompaniment. The third day was roast pork and apple sauce. And so the week went on. Just before leaving, we asked the priest if we could see his wife to thank her for the truly wonderful meals that we had eaten. He then told us that when he had important guests, his wife did not cook. Instead, he engaged the recently retired chief chef from Government House (the home of the Governor General of Rhodesia) to cook for him! He knew matters were coming to a head when he heard I was coming, so it just happened that his school bookstall burnt down ten days before we arrived for our inspection. He quoted his stocks lost at about $5,000. Unfortunately for him, the assessor was able to determine that little more than $500 had gone up in smoke.

After a long round of audits, I found it iniquitous that one priest after another was getting away with fraud and embezzlement. Bishop Cecil had clearly laid down that every layman found guilty of using funds for his own purposes was to be prosecuted in a court of law, and I had had to deal with quite a few people in this way, with former employees eventually receiving terms of imprisonment. However I was not allowed to deal with priests in the same manner, for the bishop said that that was his responsibility. Nevertheless, when I got to this priest, I felt he should not be allowed to get away with it, so I told David Neaum that I was going to ask the priest to refund those monies that I knew he had *definitely* put in his own pocket. Earning only $75 a month, there was no way that he could regularly buy himself a brand new vehicle, as he did. At the end of the week I showed him all the amounts that couldn't be accounted for, which amounted to nearly $2,000. I then told him I was going to prosecute him unless he refunded the money. No two people could have been more surprised than David and I when the priest sat down and wrote a cheque on his own personal bank account for the full amount and handed it over to me! On our long drive back to Harare we were quite sure that the cheque would bounce! Not a bit of it. The bank met the cheque in full.

The overall debts of our school system amounted to more than $60,000, and the Diocese of Mashonaland would have been bankrupted – and all priests given notice – if all our creditors had foreclosed on us. On being asked if I had any ideas on how we might extricate ourselves from the mess we were in, I suggested a centralised system of financial control with the development of a bulk-buying system (through the operation of a tender system), to provide for all the schools' requirements, right down to the last piece of chalk used in every classroom. (We needed to buy exercise books by the 'ton' – not by the gross, etc.) I was asked to draw up tentative plans to put the suggested system into operation and they were accepted by the diocese. Employment agencies were then approached with regard to finding us a suitable administrator to undertake the multi-million dollar project. On being told that such a person would require an annual salary in excess of $15,000, the diocese decided (in view of the heavy indebtedness already incurred) to ask me if I would be willing to be seconded from the full-time ministry to take on the job . . . on the understanding that it would be for a limited period (so that I would not be permanently lost to the full-time ministry), and that I would still be paid my normal priest's stipend of $130 per month ($1,560 a year), plus house and car! The Diocesan Standing Committee were a little surprised when I had the temerity to lay down two conditions before accepting the offer. First, all funds generated in the school system were to remain in the school system and the

Church would have no right to 'milk' any of the profits for any other purpose; and secondly, that I alone would have the sole right of deciding who would be hired and fired. They took a month to think about that. Next month, after accepting the conditions, I was appointed Administrator of the Diocesan Education Office. Soon afterwards I fired all the priest school managers throughout our school system and appointed full-time professional lay managers in their place. It took quite a while for the reverberations to die down!

I only lived at Ruwa for two and a half years. British sanctions were beginning to have some effect, particularly among the wealthier members of the Ruwa community who were used to drawing on large investments in the UK. The first to be affected in that connection was the Church, for a percentage of the wealthiest members decided that their 'giving' to the Church should be the first item to be trimmed drastically! When the allocation for my transport – in a large and sprawling rural area – was not sufficient for more than one day's travel in each month, there seemed to be no point in sitting round there doing very little.

We had also suffered great heartbreak in Ruwa with the crib death of our second son, David – only a month old. It was accompanied by the usual – but quite wrong – guilt feelings that perhaps we were responsible in some way. It took a long time for the pain to diminish, and for our railing against God at the injustice of it all, to cease. At first it seemed as if nothing could take away the dreadful trauma of finding a beloved child dead in his cot, but we now know that David is with God, and through our own experience have been able to help and sympathise with others facing a similar agony. By the grace of God we finally summoned up the courage to try again, and Diana was born two and a half years later. This time, for the first time, there were no traumas whatever associated with her coming into the world or with those early months. She was simply a lovely blue-eyed blonde, whose radiant personality touched the lives of everyone she was with.

Before Diana's birth we left Ruwa to live in Harare, in the parish of St Mary's, Highlands. During those spiritually barren years – while I was administrator of our education system – I helped out on Sundays as a priest when asked to do so by the rector, David Neaum. I also continued the regular Sunday 'stint', started at Ruwa, of looking after those congregations I had grown to love so much out near the north-eastern border of Zimbabwe – Mrewa, Hoyuyu and Mtoko. It was also an exhausting combination. In all I motored 40,000 miles a year, much of it over the worst bush roads in the country.

For nearly seven years I was involved with administering this enormous 'business empire', covering many hundreds of schools. It was an enormous financial success and did wonders for the Church's public relations with the Ministry of Education, parents, pupils, teachers and the business community. I couldn't help but wonder if I had at last found what God really wanted me to do.

In the school field, however, things were beginning to change. Under government policy mission schools were being pressured into moving over to come under local government control. Long before this exercise was completed, David Neaum had already begun to express increasing concern about the state of my spiritual life. He began by reminding me that my secondment had been for a limited period only, which I no longer wanted to accept. Nevertheless, with David's support, Bishop Paul asked me to return to that full-time ministry.

In a foreword to the *Education Newsletter* of January, 1975, Bishop Paul Burrough said, amongst other things:

Today probably no Anglican diocese in the world carries the responsibility for so many schools as does Mashonaland. Speaking personally, I am bound to say that when I arrived here as bishop in 1968, one of my deepest anxieties was inevitably the poor state and the indebtedness of far too many of our schools. The problems were then wonderfully overcome by the African Education Office Executive from the time that Fr John Knight was seconded to that body. Far beyond the confines of our Church, Fr Knight has been acclaimed as something of a genius in the conduct of this Christian work. It is, of course, a priestly work when so done, but the time has come when my advisers and I are quite sure that we must call Fr Knight to return to a more pastoral ministry. Inevitably this causes some dismay among our educationists ...

Reading between the lines of that statement it was obvious that they were becoming more than a little alarmed at the state of my spirituality, and were worried that I would sell myself to the 'god' of business. They were not far wrong.

In a feature article in the National Teachers' Magazine, *Forum*, of April 1975, the editor wrote:

John Knight could have been an accountant: he delights in manipulating figures and reads financial reports for pleasure. He could have been an architect: his working drawings for school extensions such as dormitories and staff houses have been adopted as standard by the Anglican Diocese of Mashonaland. He could have been a business man with a shrewd eye for a good buy and a better sell. He chose to be a priest ... and the dog-collar doesn't chafe at all. Despite his unquestioned business acumen – testified by his outstanding success as administrator and education secretary in the African Education Office of the Anglican Diocese of Mashonaland ... there has never been any conflict between it and his work as a man of God ...

How easy to pull the wool over the eyes of so many people. 'The dog-collar doesn't chafe at all' ... 'there has never been any conflict between it and his work as a man of God'. I worked hard at creating that impression, because I wanted to continue in that kind of work and *not* have to return to the full-time ministry. Obviously, to some, it was a successful gambit!

The true state of affairs in my life was that, having found real happiness in a job with tremendous job satisfaction, I was not willing to entertain the bishop's idea; my answer to him was a very determined 'NO'. The bishop was, however, persistent and said he believed God was calling me to take the post of Rector of St John's, Mutare. That made me feel uncomfortable, so I laid down several 'impossible' conditions that would have to be met before I agreed to accept the post. If they were fulfilled, I would know that it was of God and I would submit! Unbelievably, to me, all the conditions were met within the week, including the finding of a successor to take my job! I felt I could no longer say no and agreed to go.

One further thing disconcerted me about the move. I kept hearing from those in the know that Reg Clark, who had been Rector of St John's, Mutare, for twenty years had in recent times begun to face problems with a rising group of charismatics in the parish. They were doing all manner of un-Anglican things and causing the parish, so they said, a great deal of grief. It was thought that a young, energetic and hard-line traditional priest would be able to deal with the rebellion and bring the heretics back to the true faith. And that was why I was the man chosen.

Well, I had a problem here. Having been out of mainstream Church work for so long, I had no idea what or who they were talking about when they spoke of 'charismatics'. Being the kind of person who didn't like to admit he didn't know something, I couldn't ask these informers what was meant by the term. So I visited the Christian Bookshop in Harare and, pretending I knew all about the movement, asked for any books they might have about charismatics. They were as averse to them as my informants, but they did have a copy of Dennis Bennett's book *Nine O'Clock in the Morning*.

I have to admit that I went home and started reading it, but never got more than halfway through before I threw it into the corner of the room with the comment 'What rubbish!' Jill pricked up her ears, retrieved it from the corner, and she too started reading it. She too could not finish the book, and agreed heartily with my assessment. At least we thought we now had some conception of who the 'charismatics' were, and we were both agreed on what we thought of the movement before moving off to Mutare to start our new work there. We might be filled with trepidation and misgivings about going back into full-time ministry, but we both knew that the charismatic errors had to be firmly dealt with, and those who had 'deviated' brought back into the true fold of the Anglican Church.

What a wonderfully developed sense of humour God must have. How often He must chuckle over the antics we get up to – knowing that He will eventually allow the scales to fall from our eyes so that we might see how often we have been out on a limb! I went to Mutare and received a great welcome – and, of course, played it tough for six months with the 'charismatic bunch'. Mercifully small in number, I thought; thank goodness the contamination hadn't spread too far. I made a point of pretending to listen to them even though they were obviously a little round the bend. I did, however, give them a fair amount of freedom to experiment with some forms of worship, just to show them that their ideas didn't work out in practice. But all through that time God was working on *me*! These people were very loving, and most persistent (I saw them as persistent troublemakers) in their love towards me. They kept on handing me new books in the hope that, as they saw it, I would see the light. All those books irritated me as much as Dennis Bennett's had, yet for a time I read them and then returned them – usually with little or no comment because I didn't think I would be able to restrain myself from blowing a gasket.

I finally made a pact with myself. If I hadn't done something, a previous ulcer condition might well have soon reared its ugly head again. Every time 'they' offered me another book to read, I'd say 'Thank you very much', put it on one side for a fortnight, and then return it unread. If they tried to draw me on what I thought about a book, I would simply say I was still digesting what I had read! A small white lie, but essential for my continued peace of mind, I thought.

One other thing annoyed me a good deal when I arrived in Mutare. On my staff was a young priest from Ireland. I liked him instantly, and was very pleased when he agreed to stay on as my assistant priest. On the day that I was inducted as the new rector of the parish he, out of the kindness of his heart, gave me a little gift as a memento of the occasion. You can immediately understand the insecurity I felt in my ministry when I tell you that I was angered when I read the title of that gift. It was a book called *The Normal Christian Life* by Watchman Nee. It was almost as if he was insinuating I still needed to discover what the 'normal' Christian life was all about! But far worse was to follow.

I had left the book by my bedside so that I might read it when I had a moment. A night or two later I picked it up and started to read. I found I couldn't even understand what the first page was all about! That really made me mad, so I put the book down and tried to forget about it. A few weeks later, thinking that I must have been tired the first time I tried to read it, I tried again. The result was the same! I put the book away in a drawer and decided to put it out of my mind. All this did nothing for my confidence or my ego!

SIX

ASSURANCE OF A PLACE IN GOD'S KINGDOM

Soon after arriving in Mutare I was invited to attend the weekly fellowship evening of the 'charismatic' group. My immediate inclination was to decline, but on second thoughts, I decided it would be far better to know what they were getting up to, and to be available to correct incorrect teachings and interpretations from the Bible. That they were 'on fire' for the Word of God was an understatement. Instead of regarding Bible Study as a duty, they sometimes spent hours every day simply enjoying and sharing the things they had discovered with one another, and they loved long exuberant periods of worship. Oh yes! I was appalled and embarrassed at such enthusiasm, and especially at all the clapping of hands and lifting up of arms! There were also informal groups where they actually seemed to enjoy spending long periods in prayer, together, on other days of the week. I often found their fellowship evening tiring and exhausting. Instead of limiting their Bible Study – like most other reasonable groups I knew – to about an hour, it was not unusual for it to continue for a good two hours and more before refreshments were brought on. And I had a king-sized complex about what I *thought* they were saying about me. Because they continually referred to things like 'the baptism of the Holy Spirit' and 'speaking in tongues', I believed they were, in effect, saying that I was not a proper Christian, and that without the experience that they had had, I was very much a second-class citizen. All that only increased my anger and belligerence towards them. I began to look upon them, subconsciously at least, as 'the enemy' – a group that seemed to be ridiculing the spiritual leader set over them by their bishop.

But why was it that 'the enemy' had all those things that I so longed for? They simply loved the times of worship – times which I so often regarded as a duty. When extra times of worship were imposed on me, I looked upon them – unlike these people – as an extra chore and an infringement on the times I wanted to have for myself. There was also their undoubted love for the study of God's Word. Because they spent so much time on it, they were able to quote freely from the Bible from memory, and appeared to have a thoroughly good grounding in the Bible as a whole. Even after fourteen years in the ministry, much of it squandered because I could never read the Bible with the excitement of reading a novel, as they seemed to do, I still knew so little of it, and certainly did not find it easy to find a particular passage when I wanted it. Yet 'they' seemed to do so with ease. And they prayed out loud in public with such fluency, using their own ordinary everyday words! I had never found it easy to pray out aloud, and when I did, I used one of the beautifully written prayers from a prayer book. But it was the *personal* way in which they spoke to 'their Father' and to 'Jesus' that really shattered me, speaking to Him as if that person was right there with them. And they seemed to have no problem with expecting God to work miracles in their day to day situations. Their love for Jesus, so reminiscent of that personal love for Jesus my mother revealed when I was a child, was as real as the love one bears a dear personal friend on earth. It seemed to bring a living reality to their faith that affected every part and every moment of their lives.

How was it that these people, who were apparently (in much of the established Church's eyes) so off-beam as regards the 'true' teaching of the Church, had such a personal living relationship with Jesus? How was it that they radiated a joy and seemed to speak of, and experience, a power of God working in their lives that was comparable with the power and enthusiasm of the New Testament Church? How was it that they enjoyed times of prayer, worship and reading of the Bible in a way I had never found to the same extent in anyone else – and certainly not in

myself? Of course there couldn't be anything in it. As soon as
biblical phrases like 'every tree is known by the fruit it bears'
(Luke 6:44) began to surface in my mind, they had to be
hurriedly silenced.

About two months after I arrived in Mutare an incident at
one of these weekly gatherings made a very deep impression
on me. A young mother gave her testimony of what God had
been doing in her life, and of how members of the group had
prayed for her and she had been 'filled with the Holy Spirit'
the week before. She spoke of the way Scripture had 'come
alive' for her that week, as if God had been speaking directly
to her and her situation. More than that, she related several
miracles she had prayed for – mainly for her children and for
situations at home – which had all been 'provided' in
wonderful ways. It was the radiant joy, happiness and peace
on that person's face that made me realise that she was
speaking of something that had, to her, really happened and
had transformed her life.

There was another remarkable fact concerning the com-
position of this group. They were not apparently a group of
mad individuals from the lunatic fringe of the Church. They
came, by and large, from the central core of the Church's
long-standing membership. Among them were people who
had been deeply involved in the life and work of the Church
for years – but who had always wanted something more.
They had been praying for a revival in the Church, and quite
suddenly it had begun to happen to one after another of
them. From the very outset they had tried to share 'their'
experience with the leadership of the Church – and been
repelled. Yet they had the tenacity not to give up, and
continued to show love to them and pray that many others
would be brought to share this experience with them.

And it seemed, surprisingly to me, to have touched people
of all ages – and not just the impressionable young. There
were people in the group who had been Anglicans for forty,
fifty and even sixty years! There was one person we knew to
be in her nineties (although she would never own up to that)
praising the Lord just like the rest of them! Nothing would
prevent any of them from attending their groups, and times
of Sunday worship, unless it really was of the utmost import-

ance, and then only for a reason which they believed God would undoubtedly accept as a valid one.

Their faith, and their putting of it into practice, had become the most important thing in their lives. Could these really be considered the marks of heresy?

During that first year, one of our church councillors went overseas on holiday with his wife. Giles Wakeling was the son of a clergyman, with brothers and uncles who were bishops and clergymen. He was, therefore, well equipped to understand the kind of life a clergyman led, and the kind of pressures that are brought to bear on him – and on members of his family – and the financial difficulties that result from small and often inadequate stipends. Fortunately for us, he soon became one of our churchwardens and remained so for the rest of my time in the parish.

Jean and Giles had a good holiday overseas, but almost spoilt it, for me at least, when he turned up on his first Sunday back and said to me, 'Here's a book I picked up overseas. I think you might like to read it!' Although he was not, to my knowledge, 'one of them', he appeared to be open and sympathetic to their ideas. Irritation began to rise up in me as I stuffed the book into my cassock pocket and went into church.

To this day I don't know why I broke my resolution that morning. Except, of course, that God obviously intervened! After church, as I wandered across the grounds to my house, I felt the weight in my pocket, pulled the book out, and began to read it without thinking about what I was doing. I couldn't believe it! The first two or three pages were a blueprint of my own life. An unbelievable excitement began to well up within me, and by lunch-time I had stormed right through the book and my excitement had been raised to fever pitch. 'That's what I have been looking for – that's what I want.' With Jill calling the family to lunch, I only had a moment or two to kneel down and say to Jesus: 'I am wholly yours. Fill me to overflowing with your Holy Spirit, and confirm in me now that absolute assurance that I am a child of yours and that you have already guaranteed me a place in heaven. Thank you and praise you for opening my eyes at last'.

The book? The first book written by Colin Urquhart, *When*

the Spirit Comes. What a debt of gratitude I owe to Colin for having the courage to reveal his failures as a priest so that I could relate to them, and for pointing the way out! And like 'them' – that is the people who had rammed so many books down my throat – I soon obtained ten copies of Colin's book and was passing them round the parish as fast as I could! I felt so sure that everyone would discover what I had now discovered. I was largely disappointed. For a while, I failed to see that I too had not seen the truth in the past, even when it was staring me in the face. I was finally brought to understand that a 'Damascus-road' experience will come to different people, in different ways, and at different times. We have to accept the fact that until the Holy Spirit has completed His work of preparation in each individual, *as an individual*, there is no way that we can force that experience on anyone else.

The family could not understand why I looked like a Cheshire cat who had found a never-ending supply of cream. For days, I just could not contain my joy. Oh yes, I still had problems. Because of my natural reserve and embarrassment at making a spectacle of myself, there was no way that anyone was going to get me to clap or raise my hands. I still found it difficult to pray out loud – in my own words – in public. But I soon crashed through that 'sound barrier', and what a joy it brought me to gain confidence in praying openly, and more and more naturally. It became easier as I realised that I was actually speaking to someone who loved and cared for me; but even more than that – I now knew that He was intimately involved in every facet of my life and of the lives of those around me. A bumper sticker with the slogan 'Wherever you are, God is' suddenly took on new relevance to me. Instead of a relationship between a God-figure who was far away out there, and little lonely me who was here, He was, in fact, with me everywhere – even if I was, for example, sitting in a cinema watching an erotic X-rated film! Jesus wouldn't like that – and that put a whole new perspective on life! Although I had not intended it, it was almost as if I behaved one way in church – because I was in the presence of God – and quite another once outside the church. No wonder the Psalmist says that even if we travel to the ends of the

earth, or try to hide in the dark, we can never escape from
God. I knew that God was delighted when I told Him of my
love and gratitude, of my cares and concerns, of my fears and
anxieties, and of my hopes and disappointments. Intercon-
nected with this was an almost ceaseless desire to sing God's
praises – which I did. Within weeks I had learnt literally
dozens of 'Scripture' songs and these, together with many of
the great hymns of the Church, were constantly on my lips.
Suddenly verse after verse from the Bible was being im-
printed on my memory through the medium of song.

Probably the greatest breakthrough at this period, and
it was a specific answer to prayer, came in the area of
'Scripture'.

SEVEN

A WHOLE NEW WAY OF LIFE

I have already confessed to the fact that my knowledge of Scripture, despite fourteen years in the ministry, was not all that it should have been. Of course one could cover oneself by adding, 'But no one can know everything there is to know in the Bible' and in so doing create the overall impression that one is as knowledgeable as a priest, for example, could expect to be! So I need to be absolutely frank and honest by admitting that I was ashamed and appalled by my lack of knowledge in this area. I was little better than the average person who sat in most pews in most churches on a Sunday morning (whether it be in a Roman Catholic, Anglican, Presbyterian or Methodist Church, although Baptists and Pentecostals seem to be better versed in their knowledge of the Bible!) As a priest, I had learnt all the tricks of staying one step ahead of the average lay person in this area; and through admissions made to me, I have since discovered that it is true for large numbers of priests and pastors. How do we do it? Simple. When floored with a difficult question, one parries it with something like this: 'Jimmy, I am glad you brought that up and I would like to speak with you about it. Unfortunately I have to rush off to another engagement just now, but what about tomorrow . . . next week' (the next appointment being far enough away for one to do the necessary research). Or in a group – 'That is a very important subject – but would you mind, Audrey, if I just finish this topic we've been discussing, and then we will raise it at the end of the evening.' Then you make sure the evening is 'filled' and at the end you say something like – 'Oh, Audrey, dear me, we almost forgot your question. I think everyone would agree it's too late to discuss it now. Let's leave it until our next meeting and I'll make sure we deal with that issue first of all. But please, Audrey, if you feel it can't wait, do come round and see me tomorrow. Just chat to me afterwards, or give me a ring tomorrow if you are anxious about this, and we can make an appointment.' Or one floors the questioner with some big words and an offer he can't refuse. 'Peter, I am delighted that you have raised this because the whole subject of eschatology and the Parousia have been in the forefront of my mind for some time. Over and over again, during my visits around the parish, I have heard similar questions asked, all showing how much our people want to know more about this. So I'll let you into a little secret. I'm starting a six-week course of sermons at the Sunday morning service at the beginning of July. Will that meet your need, Peter?'

In most average congregations or parishes, in my experience, there are seldom more than one or two Bible Study groups a week. Thus it is possible for the average clergyman or pastor to keep a week or two ahead of these groups and foresee the likely difficulties that might arise. I had never found any problem with doing that before, but St John's in Mutare was a totally new scene. There were a number of gifted and enthusiastic lay leaders and in our first year, we had fourteen separate weekly Bible Study groups in operation. It would have been all right if they were all studying the same subject, but they weren't. Every group was different. Some were studying different books of the Bible, including Daniel, Revelation, Job and John's Gospel, and others were concentrating on particular subjects or themes in the Bible. I was not leading any of them. My role? To go round occasionally to each group. That could be taxing enough, but here was the real crunch. As a group came to the end of their particular course of study, the leader would invite me to attend the last meeting of the course and then seek answers for all the difficult problems the group had been unable to resolve for themselves – the 'expert' coming in to finalise it all!

I knew I was totally ill-equipped to deal with that. Up went the cry for help: 'Lord, you know how little I know about the Bible. Please give me a love for your Word and a deep desire to read and study it. And please allow the Holy Spirit to bring understanding to those passages that I find difficult, and reveal the deeper truths that lie hidden beneath the well-known and familiar passages of the Bible. May your Word really be a lamp to guide me, and a light for my path. Lord, forgive me for all the time I have already wasted. You know how urgent this is. Please make time for me to catch up.'

No sooner had I prayed, than God began to answer. The very next morning I woke at 3 a.m. – fresh and wide awake. After a time of prayer and worship, I found I just could not wait to get stuck in, and for two-and-a-half to three hours, I studied the Bible. That became the pattern of my life for a number of years, but the miracle of it all, to me, was that each time one of the groups threw me a difficult question I would find that, without any foreknowledge on my part, the Holy Spirit had led me to study that actual problem within the previous week, so that it was fresh in my mind. How gracious our Father is! Not that I used that to protect my 'image' or to give the impression that I could be praised in any way for my abilities. Not at all. The Holy Spirit had convicted me that I had to be open and honest and reveal to each group my lack of knowledge. I would also explain, where necessary, when God had led me to study 'their' particular difficulty days before I found myself needing to give an answer – so that all the praise was rightly ascribed to God.

One further joy that was given to me concerning this love and thirst for God's word in the Bible was a burgeoning ability to be able to find the passages that I needed, and to remember chapter and verse for a growing number of biblical quotations. That too was a gift from God, because I had never been able to retain more than a few verses at a time or for any period.

There was one practical issue that had to be dealt with. I was, at first, scandalised at the way people wrote in their Bibles, underlining passages and so on. God soon showed me that rather than being a holy object that has to be kept in an impeccable condition it is to be looked upon as a workshop manual – still holy, but to be studied and worked through as one would a set of notes! I soon found that the actual habit of underlining words and paragraphs, and the writing of notes and cross-references in the margin, helped to imprint those passages on my mind – and also helped me to find them again with greater ease.

The day I read Colin Urquhart's book was the day I came to recognise as my rebirth – when I was, in the words of Scripture, 'Born over again'. Not surprisingly that description causes problems to many people, particularly in the Church leadership. The phrase had previously made me boil with rage when someone who had been a long-standing member of the Church suddenly declared that he, or she, had just been 'born again'! 'What on earth do you think you've been doing in the Church during the last ten, twenty or thirty years?' I would ask with some sarcasm.

All through my life I had been struggling to be good enough for God, trying my best to please Him. All through that time I continually *hoped* that I would finally be good enough to go to heaven when I died. The chance of doing so seemed marginal. Was that why Jesus said that the road to hell is so wide and many follow it – and that the way to heaven is narrow, and so very few enter God's Kingdom? Added to this was yet another passage of Scripture that disturbed me. It was the one where Jesus seemed to be saying that, as in an examination, there is a percentage passmark that you have to achieve if you are going to make the grade; but the passmark laid down by Jesus seemed to be impossible for *anyone* to achieve. It was this: 'Be ye perfect, as your Father in Heaven is perfect'. I still hoped against hope that somehow I would make the grade; however, each fresh sin, and each falling back into sin, would leave me with a renewed sense of hopelessness.

But would a God who loved us allow us to go all through life struggling 'to make the grade', continually striving and continually failing, continually wondering if we would ever get to heaven? That did not smack of love! I had recently 'discovered' a verse in the Bible that I must have read literally dozens of times before without realising the full impact of what it was saying. It was this (the italics are mine): 'These things I have written to you who believe in the

name of the Son of God, *in order* that you may *know* [not hope
for] that you *have* eternal life' (John 20:31, NASV). These
assurances were of something that was a present certainty –
not just a future hope.

Then there were the words 'Believe on the Lord Jesus
Christ, and thou shalt be saved, and thy house' in Acts 16:31
(KJV). To me, everything hinged on the meaning of that
word 'believe', because there is another passage of Scripture
that says: 'Do you believe that there is only one God? Good!
The demons also believe – and tremble with fear' (James
2:19). And no devil – even though he has an *intellectual* belief
in God – is ever going to go to heaven because he 'believes' in
God. So the word 'believe' in that first passage from Acts
16:31 must involve much more than *an intellectual acceptance* of
God! So what does it mean?

What Colin's book was saying was that after years of
struggling to be good enough for God, he had suddenly come
to realise that Jesus Christ had already paid the full purchase
price of all his sins and – because of what Jesus had accomplished so perfectly for him on the Cross of Calvary – he was
now a *son of God*! By accepting that Jesus had already done
everything that was necessary to restore him to a right relationship with God, he was now assured of a place in God's
Kingdom for ever. 'All we like sheep have gone astray; we
have turned every one to his own way; and the Lord hath laid
on *him* the iniquity of us all' (Isa. 53:6, KJV).

For the first time I began to understand the relevance of
the story of Jesus and Nicodemus for the Christian Church
today. The story, in St John's Gospel, Chapter Three, is so
well-known and so obviously directed against the day-to-day
practice of the Jewish 'religion' in Christ's day – that most of
us fail to realise its significance for the *Church as it is today*.

Nicodemus was a well-known leader of the Jewish
'Church'. He had done everything a devout Jew was required
to do. He had gone through all the required initiation rites
(like our baptism, confirmation, ordination) for a man who
was to be set apart by God as a Pharisee and a leader of the
Jews. He was one of the leading exponents of the Jewish faith,
well versed in all that had to be taught to his people if they
were to fulfil the requirements of God, find favour with God,

and be His children for ever. As a Pharisee he was recognised as more devout than any other Jewish group. He tithed everything he had to God. He never missed 'going to church', and frequently took a leading part in it. We would not expect any less of priests, ministers, pastors and bishops today. Yet despite his 'worthiness', despite the seeming correctness or indelibility of his 'ordination', and despite his ministry as an accepted and recognised teacher and exponent of the faith, he had a problem.

He didn't want the crowds to know that he had doubts about his 'ordination'! He did not want to rock the boat by letting them know that he was beginning to question whether or not he was teaching the full truth as revealed in Scripture. So he went to find Jesus under the cover of darkness. Why approach Jesus? Because this man, despite the astounding fact that he had never had any training at a recognised Jewish 'theological college', was a man who spoke with an unchallengeable authority. Indeed he spoke and taught and preached with that kind of authority and grasp of the Scriptures that, if one was honest enough to admit it, left the Scribes and Pharisees floundering, and made them look ridiculous in one encounter after another. More than that, whereas they had to lay down rules in order to get people 'to church' – and most of their flock went out of a sense of duty – vast crowds simply flocked to hear Jesus wherever He went, and were willing to travel many miles over dusty roads to do so. But the really important factor was this: Nicodemus could not help but note, with astonishment, all the 'signs and miracles' that accompanied the ministry of Jesus; and certainly nothing like this had happened for several hundred years within 'the Church'. It was a long time since there had been any prophet 'working miracles'.

But with Jesus, there was an apparently never-ending stream of people being healed. Nothing could be more embarrassing for 'the established Church'. There seemed to be no doubt about it; the deaf heard, the blind saw, the dumb spake, the cripples walked, withered arms and legs were restored, the lepers were cleansed, and even the dead – if all the stories were to be believed – were raised to life. It seemed, in fact, that there was just no area of life into which Jesus did not fail to bring healing. Even epileptics were healed, and mad people and the like restored to sanity. So why was the ministry of Jesus so power-full, and the recognised ministry of 'the Church' so power-less? All of them taught from the same Scriptures, didn't they? How was it, then, that there was such a difference between them? Nicodemus knew he had to try and find the answer.

He at least, unlike the rest of his Pharisee brothers, had the courage – albeit under cover of darkness – to go and tackle Jesus over the issue. Naturally he found it hard to get to the point that was really at issue – the validity of his own ministry in the eyes of God. But he underlines the critical part of the problem when he says to Jesus, 'Rabbi, we know that you are a teacher sent from God.' Why? Because 'No one could perform the *miracles* you are doing *unless* God were with him' (John 3:2). What he wanted to say, but perhaps couldn't summon up the courage to ask, was: 'Why is my "ordained" ministry power-less, whereas your un-ordained ministry (as far as the Church is concerned) is filled to overflowing with a living demonstration of God's power-filled life?' And even though Nicodemus never actually voiced his question, Jesus *knew* that this was at the heart of what was 'burning him up'. I don't believe it would be stretching the biblical record too far to say that here was a Pharisee who had set out to devote his whole life to God, and found himself a failure – in many respects – in this area of his ministry. He was, deep down, broken-hearted by it. How true is that for all too many ministers and preachers of the Gospel today? It was certainly true of me.

But Jesus, with those gifts of knowledge, wisdom and discernment that were so much a mark of His ministry, hits at the very heart of Nicodemus' problem by the reply that He makes: 'I am telling you the truth; no one can *see* the Kingdom of God *unless* he is *born again.*' There follows the seemingly facetious reply from Nicodemus: 'How can a grown man be born again? He certainly cannot enter his mother's womb and be born a second time!'

What was Nicodemus really saying? I believe it was something like this: 'Are you telling me that I must get up in the pulpit next week and admit to all my people that after all

my college education, "ordination", and years of preaching,
I myself have failed to understand the most important issue
of all – the key to eternal life? Are you telling me that I must
go back into the womb and start all over again?' Every person
understands how difficult it sometimes is to admit publicly
that one is wrong. How much more difficult for leaders to
confess that they have made such a grievous error of judgement that the majority of their followers will die! And that
WAS the judgement of Jesus on Nicodemus and on much of
the leadership of the Church of His day. They were the blind
leading the blind, and Jesus was telling Nicodemus what
would be required from him if his ministry was to change for
the better. He needed to eat humble pie and publicly admit
he had been wrong, and to allow God to enter in and
radically change his own life!

Poor Nicodemus! (Poor John Knight!) But the problem
that had developed was not entirely his fault. For over four
hundred years there had not been a single word of prophecy
from the Lord to Israel! The 'Church' had moved away from
God. It was still going through all the motions it had been
going through for centuries – but with no sign of miracles and
wonders as in the days of the great prophets such as Elijah
and Elisha. All the initiation ceremonies were still the same.
Nicodemus, like so many generations before him, simply
taught and passed down to others what had been handed
down to him. They tried to do all the things that the laws of
the Church required. The initiation ceremonies were strictly
adhered to; they went to 'church' when it was required of
them; they gave their gifts and offerings for the work of the
Church; some even tithed everything they had. Just like so
many people in so many churches of so many denominations
today. But the majority – although doing everything that 'the
Church' required – did not have any *assurance* of eternal life,
or of how to receive it. For most, their religion only affected a
tiny part of their lives. It had not brought them to a *radical*
commitment of their lives to God; it was little more than a
hobby!

They, like us, knew lots about God (about Jesus), but had
it radically changed their life-styles? No, it hadn't. And what
about us? All too many have never been taught that *the goal* of

all the Scriptures is to bring us to that point of understanding that 'all these things have been written in order that you may *know* that you *have* eternal life' (as a present possession *now*, not just some hoped-for thing in the future after we die). And Jesus confirms this truth in John 6:47 (NASV) when He says: 'Truly, truly, I say to you, he who believes *has* [not will, or may have] eternal life,' and if we have never been taught how to appropriate that gift of eternal life here and now, then we are in the position of Nicodemus – in need of being 'born again'.

That means I stop striving to be good enough for God through my own *efforts*. No amount of 'good works' will ever make me good enough; the moment I recognise that Jesus died *in order that* I might be offered free entry to heaven; the moment I *accept* that gift – then I have been 'born again'. The truth of these words finally became a living reality in my own life – and the words of this song rang through my head for months:

> It's no longer I that liveth
> But Christ that liveth in me,
> It's no longer I that liveth
> But Christ that liveth in me,
> He lives! He lives! Jesus is alive in me.
> It's no longer I that liveth,
> But Christ that liveth in me!

> (Composer Unknown)

That new-found certainty brought a wonderful joy to my life. Christ had done it all for me already. Instead of wondering and worrying for the rest of my life about whether I would ever make it to heaven or not – I could now praise God that He had already, out of His personal love for me, made it an accomplished fact in my life.

But it also left me with a deep sorrow. A sorrow concerning 'the Church' that had failed to teach me this fact in a way that could have stopped me striving so many years before. A sorrow that I, as a priest, had spent fourteen years in the ministry unaware of this truth, and therefore unable to communicate it to so many who were searching for the reality of the Gospel. It has been a tremendous consolation to me to meet up with large numbers of those I previously ministered to who have since come to an understanding of what Jesus had accomplished for them, and have accepted that gift of eternal life.

It also left me with a deep desire to teach this truth far and wide, particularly to my own brothers and sisters in the Anglican and other mainline (other than Pentecostal) Churches that have not been taught it, and all too often go to the grave wondering whether or not they will go to heaven, or imbued with a false assurance of their salvation because they have been led to believe that their good works will prove sufficient. They will not!

EIGHT

'RECEIVE THE HOLY SPIRIT'

Having had this wonderful and totally liberating experience of knowing what it was to be 'born again' – as Jesus had commanded Nicodemus to be – there was still a great yearning within me to experience an even greater outpouring of God's power on my ministry. I remembered that it was on the day of the Resurrection – as St John records it – that Jesus 'breathed' on His disciples and said 'Receive the Holy Spirit' (John 20:22). And yet it wasn't until fifty days later – on the day of Pentecost – that anything particularly dramatic took place in their lives. They knew that Jesus loved them, and had chosen them for Himself. They had ministered in His name, going out two by two and with the seventy. They had seen healings; even demons had obeyed them and gone out of people in the name of Jesus. Sometimes they had been unsuccessful, and Jesus had to tell them that some things could not be changed, except by much prayer and fasting. Even after they had deserted Him and denied Him, they had all experienced His total forgiveness. Even so, the power-filled life of Jesus was still not theirs. Yet His certain promise to them was that *when* the power of the Spirit was released in them, they would do the things that Jesus did – 'and even greater things shall ye do'.

What happened at Pentecost was a fulfilment of both an order given, and a promise made, by Jesus to them on Ascension Day – ten days before Pentecost: 'Do not leave Jerusalem, but wait for the gift I told you about, the gift my Father promised. John baptised with water, but in a few days you will be baptised with the Holy Spirit.' Furthermore, said

Jesus, 'when the Holy Spirit comes upon you, you will be filled with power' (Acts 1:4–5, 8).

And on the day of Pentecost there was the sound of a rushing mighty wind, and we are told that tongues of fire settled on the heads of each one of them and 'they were all filled with the Holy Spirit and began to talk in other languages as the Spirit enabled them to speak' (Acts 2:4). Can you imagine the scene? Jews from every part of the civilised world listening to simple, uneducated people of their own nation speaking in the languages of every nation 'about the great things that God hath done' (Acts 2:5–11)! And it wasn't only a once-in-a-lifetime-experience. A little later, on being threatened with death if they ever spoke again in the name of Jesus, they prayed for boldness to continue their God-given work: 'And now Lord, take notice of the threats they have made, and allow us, your servants, to speak your message with boldness. Stretch out your hand to heal, and grant that wonders and miracles may be performed through the name of your holy servant Jesus.' (It is remarkable that there was *no* direct prayer for their enemies to be dealt with!) 'When they finished praying, the place where they were meeting was shaken. They were all filled with the Holy Spirit and began to proclaim God's message with boldness' (Acts 4:29–31).

I, too, longed to see the Church transformed in that way. And I wanted to be a part of it so that God could transform all my failings in ministry, and give me gifts that I did not naturally have, so that I might proclaim the Good News with power. I wanted to see people's lives transformed, renewed, healed; and because these gifts would be seen to be 'supernatural' gifts, the glory would be given to God. But how to go about receiving that release of the Spirit's power within me? That was the question I wanted answered.

I knew that that lovely man of God, Bill Burnett (Bishop of Grahamstown and later Archbishop of Capetown), had simply been praying in his own home (just before Sunday lunch!) when he had suddenly discovered that he was praying easily and fluently in another tongue. There were others I had read about who had received that mark of the Spirit's baptism when people who had already received that gift laid hands on them to receive it. We were soon to discover that God is always sovereign, and that there is no set formula that can always guarantee the gift of tongues for someone seeking that gift. Sometimes it happened through the laying-on of hands, sometimes during a person's time of prayer, and sometimes quite spontaneously. On some occasions when a person had, over a period of time, sought the gift and nothing had happened, I counselled them to stop striving to get this particular gift and accept whatever gifts the Holy Spirit *had* given them. If the Lord wanted them to have the gift of tongues later, well and good! And all too often, sometimes within days or weeks, at a time when they were least expecting it, they would find themselves praying in tongues. For several people it happened in the bath!

For a number of weeks and months, I trusted the Lord to give me that gift in the privacy of my home. But nothing happened. I accepted that the Holy Spirit had always been present in my life convicting me 'of sin, and of righteousness and of judgement' (John 16:8). Even more importantly, I knew that no one could be brought to salvation unless the Holy Spirit was working in him or her. No one could call Jesus 'Lord' – that is accept His full authority in their life – unless the Holy Spirit was behind it. I knew that it was because of His presence in me that I, too, had experienced 'rebirth'. When I had been christened as an infant, the desire of my God-fearing parents was that I should come to know Jesus and surrender my life to Him. For similar reasons they had encouraged me to be confirmed when I was thirteen, and my uncle-bishop had laid hands on me and prayed 'Receive the Holy Spirit' as Jesus had done to His disciples on the day of the Resurrection. And, as with them, there had been no manifestation of the release of the Holy Spirit's *power* in my life. Of course at the time I had been well prepared not to expect a Pentecost-experience because I had been told it had only happened that way in the first days of the Church, and that such manifestations were not needed now. That was the general teaching of the Church! Perhaps that is why the Church's leadership – and so many members within the Church – have found it so difficult to talk about the person and work of the Holy Spirit. It has always been relatively easy to talk and teach about the 'persons' and roles played by God the Father and by God the Son – but the Holy Spirit has so often been something vague and nebulous to the mainline Churches (the word 'Ghost' in the English language, has not helped the situation!) All too often the Holy Spirit is referred to as 'it'! Oh, yes! We believe in the Trinity, but . . .

On a lighter level – and perhaps with more than a grain of truth – it could be said that all the mainline Churches accept the Trinity but that to a casual observer, it must often be thought that for Roman Catholics and High Church Anglicans, it is Father, Son and Virgin Mary; for some Anglicans, it is Father, Son and Prayer Book; and for evangelicals and Protestants, it is Father, Son and Holy Scripture. And no wonder that some bishops and clergy became 'very hot under the collar' when someone referred to confirmation – when we ask for the out-pouring of the Holy Spirit – as 'empty hands on empty heads'! It is an acknowledged fact that the one Sunday in the year that causes the greatest difficulty 'sermon-wise' for most preachers, is Trinity Sunday!

I eventually came to believe that what was needed in my life, for the power of the Holy Spirit to be released in me, was the laying-on of hands. This was enormously difficult for me, mainly because of my pride. Pride in my ministry as a priest, and as an ordained man of God. There is an inherent belief amongst 'the clergy' that we are expected to understand most things to do with the faith, and that we have an indelible and inherent right to minister to everyone else's needs – but at no point may the lay members of the Church minister to us! I mean, it would be about as ridiculous as an Anglican or Roman Catholic priest asking a lay person to celebrate at the Holy Communion service. It was just not on! In the ordained ministry, we are taught to look upon our ordination as something that sets us apart – and in no way can the roles be reversed.

Although I looked all round Zimbabwe, I knew of no bishop or priest who had received the gift of tongues who might have been able to lay hands on me. So I made a pact with God. I would go anywhere, South Africa or wherever, for this laying-on of hands. Why did I make that pact? Because I knew only too well that quite a number of my own

lay people already had this gift, but there was no way that I,
as a priest, was going to receive the laying-on of hands from
them! I mean, amongst other things, how would they ever
respect me as their spiritual leader again if I were to ask
them? However God began to show me that I had grievously
hurt these 'spirit-filled' people over the past months. More
than that, why should I travel hundreds, or thousands, of
miles to receive this laying-on of hands from people who
would save my dignity, when right here in Mutare there were
people God had already anointed in this special way? I began
to see that asking these lay people to do it would be a means of
putting right my past judgemental and critical attitudes. It
would be a way of saying sorry that would be deeply
meaningful to them. Nevertheless, I found that I could not
eat that humble pie! So I went on praying to God for that
'release' – but only if it happened in some other way. Nothing
happened!

I went away on our clergy retreat in January 1976. There it
was borne upon me that I had been laying down conditions
to God – and that in no way would God bestow gifts upon me
on *my* terms! It was a very painful week as I faced up to what I
believed God was telling me to do. On 19 January, 1976, the
day after my birthday, and soon after returning from the
retreat, I went into the chapel (alongside the church) where
quite a number of people met for prayer each morning. I
began to tell them of the things I believed God had been
showing me. I asked them for forgiveness for all the sorrow,
hurt and pain that I had caused them, and particularly for
my judgemental attitude. Then I explained that contrary to
all my misgivings in the past about such a ministry from lay
people, I needed to ask them to lay hands on me for the full
release of the Holy Spirit's power within me. Would they
please do so?

There followed a truly wonderful time. There was much
weeping all round that chapel as they laid hands on me and
prayed for me. And what an unbelievable experience it was!
(It might be of comfort to some to know that although several
spiritual gifts such as wisdom and knowledge were discerned
in my ministry by others over the next few years, I did not
speak in tongues for some considerable time. In fact it was

several years before I suddenly discovered that I was *singing* in tongues before the spoken tongue followed! I have often asked myself why this was. Perhaps it was a mixture of fear of the unknown, the fear of being made to look ridiculous, and the barrier of years of tradition to be broken down).

To get back to the chapel, there was no crowing over the one who had at last stumbled on the truth. Far from it. There was simply such joy at what God was doing in all our lives, that I finally recognised the deep love that these people had for me, and the deep respect they held for the 'shepherd' that God had placed over them. There was, also, an overwhelming excitement and anticipation at what God was now going to do in our community. There was such an urgent need for the power of God to be seen operating in our midst. The war in Zimbabwe against the 'guerillas' or 'freedom fighters' posed a serious and daily threat to many of our lives, and Mutare was beginning to enter a period when it would be almost completely isolated from Harare and the rest of Zimbabwe – because of the fear of ambushes along the trunk routes and line of rail.

Not surprisingly, what had happened to me soon became common knowledge. The reverberations of that action began to take effect – usually antagonistic – among the rest of the Anglican Church around Zimbabwe. It was surprising how many Anglican priests seemed to take their holiday in our part of the country over the next six to twelve months – almost as if they wanted to find out for themselves exactly what was going on! The moment I saw the interest and tried to broach the subject with them, they retreated rapidly. The only relief in the minds of some was 'thank God it has happened on the eastern border and is too far away to contaminate the rest of the Church'! Nevertheless we praise and thank God that many parishes and clergy in Zimbabwe have since experienced a similar renewal over the last twelve years.

One of the difficulties about the Holy Spirit and the Bible is that sometimes the Bible refers to the 'Person' of the Holy Spirit, and sometimes it seems to refer to the Holy Spirit as 'power'. Perhaps it is for this reason that the Holy Spirit has often been called 'it'. In English Bible translations the words

'Holy Spirit' are always preceded by the definite article *'the'*. That is not the case in the original Greek, which has either *'the* Holy Spirit' or just simply 'Holy Spirit'. The original Greek recognises two different elements. In speaking of *'The* Holy Spirit', the Greek refers to *the Person* of the Holy Spirit. In speaking of 'Holy Spirit' (without the definite article) the Greek is always referring to the *release of power* which the Holy Spirit brings about.

One example that shows this distinction appears in Luke 4:1. (The word bracketed thus: [the] does *not* appear in the original Greek): 'Jesus returned from the Jordan *full of* [the] Holy Spirit, *led* by *the* Spirit . . .' The Greek text refers to a person full of Holy Spirit *power*, being *led by* the Person of the Holy Spirit.

A quick glance through a number of references to the Holy Spirit in the New Testament produces an interesting pattern that supports this supposition. For instance, the Greek New Testament obviously refers to the *Person* of the Holy Spirit when it mentions:

i) the Holy Spirit as a teacher, or person who speaks (Luke 2:26; 12:12; John 14:26; Acts 13:2);

ii) the Person who leads or directs (Matt. 4:1; Mark 1:12; Luke 4:1(b));

iii) the Person who comes to seal a person with power (Matt. 3:16; Mark 1:10; John 1:32; 1:33a; Acts 1:8; 2:38; 19:6; Eph. 1:13; 1 Thess. 4:8).

In *all* the above examples the word 'Holy Spirit' is *always* preceded by the definite article.

But when the Greek text refers to Holy Spirit as *power*, the Greek for Holy Spirit is *never* preceded by the definite article 'the'. For example:

a) when referring to people being filled with Holy Spirit power (Elizabeth, Luke 1:41; Simeon, Luke 2:25; Jesus, Luke 4:1(a); John Baptist, Luke 1:15,17);

b) when Mary's conception is spoken of as Holy Spirit power at work in her (Matt. 1:18; 1:20; Luke 1:35);

c) when a person is filled or baptised with Holy Spirit power (Acts 1:5; 2:4; 4:31; 10:38; 19:2) and when Holy Spirit power is given to those who ask for it (Luke 11:13);

d) in speaking of Jesus as the one who baptises in Holy

Spirit power (Matt. 3:11; Mark 1:8; John 1:33(b); John 20:22); and

e) when Holy Spirit power within oneself can witness with one's own spirit (Rom. 9:1).

Strangely enough I had a similar linguistic problem when I set off to preach at the prison in Mutare. I shared this prison ministry with a black pastor and good friend, Enrose Hwata. I explained to him on one particular morning, as we were going to the prison, that I was going to preach on the theme of the Holy Spirit, and that amongst other things I wanted to bring out the distinction the Bible shows between 'the Person' and 'the power' of the Holy Spirit. Enrose, fortunately, pointed out to me that the Shona language (used by the majority of the prison inmates) would present yet another problem. They have *no* definite article in their language. So, in the same way as with the English translations, no distinction is made in the Shona Bible translation between the two different references to Holy Spirit. Whereas English translated both 'meanings' as '*the* Holy Spirit', the Shona language translated both as simply 'Holy Spirit'. (So in neither of these languages is this subtle, but important, distinction brought out.) Having at first thought I would have to leave out the meaning of this important distinction, I believe God came to my aid and gave me an analogy that, though not perfect, helped me to show those prisoners that the translators had overlooked something that really was quite important.

I asked those men to consider the word 'Night'. It would, I said, immediately bring to mind such thoughts as moon, stars, and darkness. But if I were to add the simple little prefix of 'Mr' to it – 'Mr Night' (the way most Africans invariably spelt my name!) the whole meaning would be changed. One would no longer think of moon and stars, but of a person. Such a small addition can mean so much. And it is this subtle distinction in the original Greek New Testament that has been overlooked by so many.

For a long time I used an English translation of the Bible – at the suggestion of David Pawson – where I had systematically crossed out the word 'the' in front of 'Holy Spirit' whenever it did not appear in the Greek New Testament. It has helped my understanding of the context of the passage.

Unfortunately my baptism in the Spirit caused consternation not only in the wider Anglican Church, but also in the other non-Pentecostal Churches in Mutare, and particularly amongst members of my own congregation. It caused a great deal of hurt simply because it was felt that I had gone over and joined 'the rebels' – despite my being sent to bring the rebels back into line again. I had gone over to 'their' side. This also disrupted and strained the relationship between Jill and myself. Jill, too, was longing to find a deeper relationship with God, but had not experienced – at that time – what I had done. The grievous hurt of not being understood sent us both off to find refuge and comfort in the company of like-minded people. It proved to be a long time before we both came to a full experience of the same things, and before full healing could be brought into our relationship.

The immediate accusation could perhaps be summarised something like this: 'How could I betray all that I had stood for in the Anglican Church?' How it affected my ministry in Mutare – and particularly in St John's – will be dealt with next.

NINE

POWER OF GOD IN TRANSFORMING ATTITUDES

When we arrived in Mutare in 1975, there was already a fair amount of ferment over the use of a recent South African Experimental Liturgy, rather similar to Series One in England, which was used alternately with the Central African Prayer Book. This new liturgy, referred to as the 'Orange Book' because of the colour of the cover, was introduced during the time of my predecessor, Canon Reg Clark. They had also experienced the introduction of guitars and an African drum, but this normally only happened at special services aimed at young people. That generation of gifted musicians had, by and large, moved off to universities and higher colleges of education. Up until a short while after my arrival, the church was packed on Sunday mornings with all the Anglican boarders from two high schools who were obliged to attend church whether they liked it or not. Many attended with very bad grace and showed it by the way they behaved. Fortunately, unlike my predecessor, I arrived in time to see the schools alter that plan. Instead, pupils attended church on a voluntary basis, or attended the special services arranged for them within the schools. When they left, it made one realise how thin the ranks really were in church on a Sunday morning. We had to start building!

At St John's there were, and are, essentially two major groups of people amongst the regular worshippers: those who attend the early 7 a.m. service (by and large containing a very much older age group, and much more 'traditional' in their outlook); and those who attend the 9.15 a.m. service (mostly young families, together with the majority of those who have experienced the 'baptism', 'infilling' or 'renewal' of the Holy Spirit). The 9.15 group has always been much more amenable to change. There was a third much smaller group that supported the traditional Evensong and a fourth group that consisted of those who attended the Shona-speaking afternoon service. Canon Reg Clark and the Church Council had so arranged the use of liturgies that the Prayer Book and 'Orange Book' alternated Sunday by Sunday at the two services so that, by changing one's time of attendance, there was always one service to cater for everyone's taste *each* Sunday. However, as many of our members did not attend every Sunday – and so could not remember which service had which liturgy on which Sunday – *every* Sunday without fail we had irritated, annoyed, or downright angered people present because they had come to the service they couldn't abide! This was certainly not very conducive to creating a spirit of harmony or the right attitudes for worship! I can always remember laughing at people's descriptions of seeing smoke issuing from the ears of those who are fuming. I soon found it to be only too true. You can pick them out with ease. The 'temperature' of a congregation wanting to glorify God in the presence of even a small pocketful of resentment cools rapidly. Satan revels in that!

I therefore came into a situation that was already causing many 'prickles'. We thought we had hit on a brainwave – after a referendum in the congregation some months later – when, instead of alternating liturgies between the services on Sundays, we agreed to have the Prayer Book service at the 7 a.m. service, and the 'Orange Book' at 9.15 a.m. The vast majority of those who came early were the people who loved the traditional ways. You can never please everyone all the time, and some people who didn't like getting up early, but who really were antagonistic to anything modern, decided to leave the Church. It's reminiscent of the argument over which translation of the Bible should be used in church. One great supporter of the King James, or Authorised Version was so incensed at the introduction of a twentieth century translation that he was heard to say, in defence of tradition, 'If the Authorised was good enough for St Paul, it's good enough for me'! If Paul was anything like the speaker, he

would have been appalled at the Scriptures being translated from the original Hebrew and Greek! It needs to be
said that though some were strongly 'trad' or 'modern',
the large part of our congregation were happy with either
liturgy, and many moved regularly from one service to the
other.

At the height of the guerilla war we had another invasion of
school children. This time it was the girls of St David's
Secondary School, from the Anglican Mission at Bonda,
forty-five miles out on the road to Nyanga. The school was
moved into the empty Dominican Convent in Mutare for
security reasons. The invasion of several hundred, well-
disciplined girls on a Sunday morning – split between the two
main services – presented the church with a seating problem.
For the first time I came across a *new* excuse for people
leaving a Church: 'The church is too full for comfort'! They
couldn't face being cheek-by-jowl with others in the pew. If
the truth be known, and this has to be admitted, they didn't
like 'their' church being swamped by other races, and moved
to another denomination whose congregation was still all-
white.

All through our time at St John's we had a multi-racial
congregation. For most of that time we had about a third
each of blacks, coloureds and whites. No coloureds seemed to
attend the 7 a.m. service, and very few blacks. Many of those
who had, admitted they didn't try again because the 7 a.m.
congregation seemed to ignore them after the service, and
they didn't feel welcome. It is also true to say that the black
and coloured races tend to prefer more lively services. The
7 a.m. certainly wasn't that, although it was a worshipful
service that *I* appreciated. It was a deliberate policy *not* to
change things at that service. It was intended for those who
liked the Prayer Book Service, preferring the more traditional hymns to those composed in the latter part of this
century. These people liked a service to be taken 'in the way it
had always been done'. I promised to honour those views and
practices as far as possible. It needs to be said that there was
always a steady trickle of people moving from the 7 a.m. to
the 9.15 – scurrying back in shock after the first time or two –
and yet eventually finding that they liked the new service,

and the spontaneous joy and happiness they found expressed in that service. By and large they were the people who had first been drawn into the house groups, and had found many of their preconceived ideas, inhibitions and attitudes dealt with there.

There were two 'High Church' congregations (referred to by some as 'smells and bells' because of the use of incense and bells) in the satellite towns of Sakubva and Dangamvura, but St John's was the only Anglican church serving the city centre and its own extensive and sprawling suburbs. For this reason we had to try and cater for a wide range of church-manship – particularly amongst the whites who had come from many different traditions. (Historically the Anglican Church in Zimbabwe has been strongly Anglo-Catholic with no provision, apart from one or two notable exceptions, for those of an Evangelical persuasion.) Inevitably St John's was unable to please all the people all the time. It is a sad reflection on us that our churchmanship frequently brings out our selfishness and intolerance of others to their different, but equally deeply held, ideas about the ordering of services.

Speaking of attitudes, we had a problem at St John's because the coloured people always sat at the back of the church. Only as we became more open and honest with each other did we discover the reason for this. Years before, because there was no church building for the coloured people to worship in at Florida – the area they were relegated to live in at that time – the white congregation allowed them to come to St John's on the understanding that i) they sat at the back of the church and ii) (because a common chalice was used) they received their communions at the end! (Just like feudal times in the West!) Despite this appalling insult to them as an ethnic group, they remained faithful to the Lord. After discovering this – and with repentance, forgiveness and healing between the two groups achieved – I was able to rib them on a Sunday morning when they continued to pack the back rows out of habit. Despite the past indignities heaped upon them, these faithful soldiers of Christ had remained, and continue to remain, faithful and devoted workers in all that the church has done, and is doing.

St John's had, on average, 250 worshippers every Sunday.
A quarter of these would be at the 7 a.m., and the majority of
the remainder at 9.15. Despite the changes that came about
in the lives of quite a large number as a result of the renewal,
there were no dramatic changes in the format of the 9.15. The
'Orange Book' was replaced by 'Liturgy '75', approved by
the bishops for a ten year period from 1975, with optional
liturgies to choose from similar to the British ASB issued a
few years later. Changes were only introduced after a period
of teaching, and then only when such change was voluntarily
implemented by the congregation. For a number of people in
the renewal, the pace of change was too slow, and sadly a
percentage of them left for other Churches. We felt it important not to empty the church of the more traditional members, but to try and carry everyone along together.

After ten years of 'renewal', apart from much greater use
of Scripture songs, the raising and clapping of hands by those
wishing to do so (never more than two-thirds at any one
time), most people feeling free to move round the church to
greet one another at the exchanging of the Peace, and
changes of emphases in the service, there was no radical
change in the 9.15. However, the last two years saw the
introduction of two distinctive features. The young people
(with guitars and tambourines) were responsible for the
preparation and leading of praise and worship times. The
significant effects resulting from this were not so much the
time spent in practising (although that is important, and
they did that), but in the fact that young people saw worship
as an essential part of ministry, and spent much time during
the preceding week *in prayer* – for the choice of music, for the
congregation, for themselves to be worthy vessels for God to
use, and particularly that the worship time would help to
bring people to a point of experiencing the Presence of Jesus.
Not that we ever experienced the same intensity as what
happened in the Temple in the time of Solomon. Yet that
story does speak of the importance of *praise and worship* in
breaking down the strongholds of the principalities and
powers of the evil one, *so that* we might indeed enter into the
Holy of Holies:

All the priests present, regardless of the group to which they belonged, consecrated themselves ... The Levites stood near the east side of the altar with cymbals and harps, and with them were a hundred and twenty priests playing trumpets. The singers were accompanied in perfect harmony by trumpets, cymbals, and other instruments, as they praised the Lord, singing: 'Praise the Lord because He is good, and His love is eternal.' *As* the priests were leaving the Temple, it was suddenly filled with a cloud shining with the dazzling light of *the Lord's presence*, and *they could not* continue the service of worship (2 Chr. 5:11–14).

The second important feature was the formation of a ministry team for the 9.15. It had two regular functions. The first was to meet half an hour before the service to pray specifically for God's anointing on every part of the service – on those who would minister, for the Word of God in readings and preaching to touch the hearts of everyone, and for people in the service to be convicted of their need for Christ; they also prayed for those who were still abed, or intent on doing something else with their Sunday – that God would convict them of their need of Him and to come and worship Him! Their second function was to be available in the chapel, alongside the church, to minister to anyone in need during the time that the Communion was being administered. Many came forward for counselling, prayers for healing and so on. Many testified to the healings that were received, many committed their lives to Christ, and many were baptised in the Spirit.

Although *we* found it hard to observe the change that was taking place – because it seemed so slow and immeasurable – those who visited us from time to time, from out of town, were more able to measure those changes and spoke of what they saw as exciting improvements since their last visit. Almost every visitor commented on the warm welcome they received, the real sense of belonging they sensed, the obvious and demonstrable warmth and love within the congregation (across all ethnic divides), the almost tangible presence of Jesus, and the relevance of every part of the liturgy to their daily lives, that they felt was achieved throughout the service.

It must be acknowledged that despite all the care that was taken not to 'rock the boat', people's feelings were often hurt and feathers ruffled. We *did* often fail because we sometimes allowed our human nature to get the better of us, and we allowed our natural enthusiasms to carry us away. The actual pace of change speaks volumes for the care and concern that those in the renewal had towards those who found change difficult to accept. It needs to be stressed that at no time was it felt everyone had to fit into the same mould, and that what *was* required was that everyone should be free to do whatever they felt was right for *them* – at any point of worship – *as they recognised that they stood in the presence of God.* What an awesome, yet wonderful, privilege that is!

The more dramatic changes in patterns of worship took place in many of the House Groups. Scripture songs, quite a number composed locally, formed the bulk of the 'renewal hymnal'. Many inhibitions and former attitudes were dealt with, through teaching and study of Scripture. The most dramatic change, for dyed-in-the-wool Anglicans like myself, was the experiencing of prophecies, speaking in tongues with interpretation, singing in the Spirit, clapping and raising of hands, dancing to the Lord, ministering to one another's needs – praying in tongues for wisdom, knowledge and discernment while doing so – and learning to discern the Holy Spirit's lead during times of worship. Having sung in choirs all my life, probably *the* most dramatic experience for me was 'singing in tongues'. Without prior preparation of what key to sing in, what part each individual would sing – indeed neither notes or words are given for people to sing – everyone simply begins to sing 'as the Spirit gives them utterance'. Far from being a cacophony of noise, or bedlam, there is not a discordant sound to be heard. I have been in a crowd with as many as 6,000 singing in this way – with as many different tunes and words – and on this occasion as on many others, it turned into the most wonderful song of praise imaginable.

I have to admit that I initially faced many problems in

these areas myself. Years of ingrained Anglican tradition
made me strongly prejudiced against much of what I saw as
unnecessary 'accretions' to a well-balanced, well-ordered
service. Was I taking refuge in a set form of service, however
carefully and wonderfully devised, because of a fear within
me about those things of which I had no personal experience,
and which St Paul obviously seemed to consider to be
essential if the Holy Spirit was to be sovereign in each
enactment of that 'form of service'? (1 Cor. 14:26–33).

Added to that, my own British reserve made it well-nigh
impossible for me to do anything that would require a public
expression of my love for God in ways that were contrary to
established Anglican norms and conventions. Nor can I
begin to describe what it did to me the first time I heard a
guitar, a trumpet, or – worst of all – a set of drums being
played in church! The sheer horror to me of such 'sac-
rilegious' instruments left me positively longing for the
ground to open up and swallow me.

When I had the gall to start voicing the horror in me,
people lovingly began to point to verses in Scripture that
showed me my feelings were nothing other than prejudice.
Why should an organ, or at second best a piano, be 'sanctified' while other instruments are not? (Trumpets, I had
thought, might just be permissible on royal occasions in very
large English minsters and cathedrals, but . . . and yet, isn't
our worship the expression of our love for the King of Kings
and Lord of Lords?) The passage from Chronicles already
quoted in this chapter speaks of a *hundred* trumpeters, plus all
manner of other musicians, used together with the singers to
glorify God. The net result was that the place was *filled* with
the glory of the Lord. Obviously *God* did not disapprove! One
of the consequences of our modern 'sanctifying' of a single
instrument is that we have denied large numbers of people
their opportunity of ministering with their God-given gifts –
playing instruments to God's glory. Instead, as we will hear
later in connection with the priestly ministry, we have given
the job of many to a single, 'professional' organist. References to instruments being used in worship almost always
speak of large numbers of them, and a considerable variety,
at that, being used together to glorify God. For example, look

at Psalm 150: 3–5. What a joy in ministry has been denied to so many!

I could get emotionally involved with many things, and with people, but put me within the four walls of a church and I became another person, with all my British reserve coming to the fore. There was only one way of behaving in a church: hushed tones relieved by occasional brief outbursts of singing if one was that way inclined. Otherwise all movement was strictly regulated by the prayer book – sitting, standing or kneeling. All other actions (leaping for joy, dancing and the like – heaven forbid!) were carefully excluded by having the pews judiciously placed to physically restrict anyone from attempting such things! (Baptists, Presbyterians and the like go a stage further and place their pews even closer together so that even kneeling is ruled out!) Was it not a fact that we considered too much enthusiasm or emotionality about the God we loved and served, and to whom we dedicated our whole lives, to be out of place in a church?

I often reveal my emotions when I attend or watch an exciting game of rugby or football, and indeed 'let my hair down', as I get as enthusiastic as the next person in supporting my team and their exploits, and jubilantly jump up and down when that seems to be appropriate. So why *not* be allowed or able to do so when one considers the quite fantastic exploits of God all down through history, together with the miracles He performs daily in our lives? Why *not* be allowed to show any special emotion when I consider what Jesus Christ did on the Cross for me, so that I might be forgiven, restored and given a place in His eternal Kingdom simply because He loved me so much? And why should I *not* show any emotion over the fact that He revealed that love while I was still a sinner? How unbelievable! Yet we have allowed a set pattern of unemotional, undemonstrative worship to be built up, and heaven help anyone who breaks those conventions. They are withered into a state of shame by the looks that are directed at them for any infringement.

I praise God for the many loving people who released me from that kind of bondage, and for showing me that Scripture is in fact filled with examples of active, demonstrative, extravagant, and passionate praise to God. In our everyday

world we often find ourselves clapping our hands to express
delight, or to show our appreciation or approval. What more
natural thing to do as a way of expressing our joy and delight
to God who does *everything* better than anyone else? It is a
much used method of praise to God in the Scriptures (Ps.
47:1, Isa. 55:12). In the same way – in Scripture – it is the
most natural thing in the world to express love and adoration
to God by raising one's hands in praise or self-surrender (Ps.
63:4). Unfortunately our reserve so often makes us fearful of
following suit! (Not because of what God would think, let it
be said, but through fear of what people around us might
think!)

We pray, because Jesus taught us to do so, 'Thy Kingdom
come, on earth *as it is in Heaven*'. Do we really want that? Do
we want to see heaven's pattern – of worship for instance –
replace ours here on earth? In Scripture we are given a
number of pictures of what worship is like in heaven; in the
well-known passage in Isaiah, Chapter Six and in those
wonderful passages given in Revelation 4:6–11; 5:8–14; 7:9–
12; 11:15–17 and 19:1–7 for example. Powerful praise and
worship indeed! However there is one thing that they do
constantly which I have never seen done in most churches I
have been in: 'After this I looked and there was an enormous
crowd – no one could count all the people . . . All the angels
stood round the throne [hundreds and millions of them we
learn in an earlier reference], the elders, and the four living
creatures. Then they THREW THEMSELVES FACE
DOWNWARDS IN FRONT OF THE THRONE AND
WORSHIPPED GOD . . .' (Rev. 7:9–11).

Our church seating arrangements tend to make that impossible! But would we if we could? What would it do to our
Sunday best, let alone what our peers would think? In
Mutare we held quite a number of all-night vigils of prayer.
Sometimes, being on my own in the chapel, I would feel the
need to prostrate myself before God, yet I still often found
myself looking over my shoulder in case someone walked in
at the wrong(?) moment and found me like that! Was that
honouring God when I was more concerned about what my
peers would think? Of course not. Is it not perhaps a sign that
we are not yet prepared to make that total abasement, and

radical commitment, of ourselves before God in the company of our fellow believers?

What about our feet? Do we use *them* to God's glory as part of our worship? In the story of the lame man who was healed when he met with Peter and John, we are told that he immediately entered the Temple – the *place of worship* – with the disciples 'walking and jumping and praising God'. The disciples never told him to stop being so exuberantly excited over a miracle in a place of worship (Acts 3:8). Dear God! Would we allow *that* in our church? Yet Scripture frequently speaks of people 'dancing' to the Lord as an expression of their joy and *excitement*. How seldom is this demonstrative joy found in any of our church services? See Psalms 30:11,12 and 150:4 for examples.

None of this denies the fact that there is also a need, when it is right, for times of solemnity. For times of weeping and sorrow as a mark of our contrition and sadness when that is appropriate; and for something else which, though remarked upon as of great importance in Scripture, is often neglected in our times of worship: the need for periods of silent adoration in the presence of the Living God! 'When the Lamb broke open the seventh seal, there was silence in Heaven for about half an hour' (Rev. 8:1).

Of all the regular worshippers over that ten year period, including the large numbers who emigrated or were subject to company transfers, probably well in excess of sixty per cent, discovered new joys, and found new dimensions, to worship they had never experienced before. They testified to the exciting changes that it brought about in their lives.

It has taken God a long time to break down many of my past attitudes to worship, and He is continuing that work within me. The Holy Spirit's aim in doing this in me, as in all of us, is that I might eventually worship God in complete freedom, 'in Spirit and in Truth'. May it be soon. Only God can do that work in us. But He also needs our willing co-operation. None of this 'over my dead body' attitude we so easily adopt!

TEN

POWER OF GOD IN CHANGING LIVES

Two people in a non-Anglican Church in Mutare, Harry and Sue, had also been part of the group that had experienced the baptism of the Holy Spirit before I arrived. They had been praying earnestly for renewal to take place in their own congregation. They had a young pastor who surprised me by coming to our Anglican weekday Communion services. He told me that during his training for the ministry, and whilst doing his degree at an Oxbridge Anglican College he had come to enjoy the opportunity of beginning the day around the Lord's Table. He became one of our most regular attenders at those weekday services. When my life was changed so dramatically, Harry and Sue asked me to share all I had experienced with their pastor. He was searching deeply all through his short time in Mutare. We had a good relationship, but he shied away from the 'baptism of the Holy Spirit'. On one occasion he came to me with an unusual request. One of his people had asked him to anoint her with oil 'for healing' and he didn't know how to go about it. Had I any experience in this field? He knew it to be scriptural, because the woman had told him that she believed that God had spoken to her through James, Chapter 5, verses 14 to 16, and she wanted the elders to do it for her. She was scarcely able to walk, and the ailment had been getting progressively worse for some time.

I admitted to him that it was a fairly regular part of our ministry, and so he asked me to carry it out on his behalf – with him taking part and observing. A number of my lay people accompanied me, and we were able to bring great joy and peace to the woman concerned. (She now takes long walks without any sign of the past illness). And although he was getting more and more interested (with occasional bouts of withdrawal), he was called to serve another church before anything happened. After the interregnum, we heard that the new pastor was a mature person who had taken early retirement from his secular job, and entered the full-time ministry. We also heard, along the grapevine, that he had experienced 'renewal'!

It was with great excitement that we welcomed his arrival. I was fairly exuberant in my welcome, and greeted him in the 'traditional' way by putting my arms around him! I immediately sensed his withdrawal, and realised that the grapevine was possibly misinformed about that renewal experience. As a result, I found Dennis keeping his distance from me in the next few months.

It was some time later that I decided, with my Church Council, to hold a mission for the young people of our church. Through our friendship with another pastor in Harare (Jill had been to school with his wife), we asked if members of his youth group – a dynamic, spirit-filled, group – could come down and conduct a mission for our own young people. They agreed to send their leaders down with a coach-load of young people for a weekend.

As it was going to involve youngsters from his own denomination in Harare we suggested to Dennis that he might like to bring along his young people. Without being over-enthusiastic about the idea, he did finally agree that his young people could take part in the weekend. The mission was a wonderful success. Many of our young people were born again. All of them, without exception, were set on fire for Christ. At the end of the weekend, both Dennis and I discovered that we had been thinking the same thing – 'what a pity to break our young people up into two separate groups after all they had experienced together'! So, against all expectations, Dennis and his wife Shirley, and Jill and I became co-leaders of a combined 'YP' (Young People or, as we called it 'Youth Praise') group.

All went well until Dennis and Shirley went away on holiday. One Friday evening a number of young people –

several from Dennis' Church – said that they wanted to have
the laying-on of hands so that they could receive the baptism
of the Holy Spirit. Realising that I found myself in a tricky
situation, I had to mark time until Dennis had been con-
sulted, and so I told them that I was not prepared to do that
until they had had some teaching on the subject. This, at
their insistence, we started to do during the next couple of
weeks while Dennis was still away. However, as soon as he
returned, I visited him and told him about the request and
what I had done about it. Dennis immediately asked me to
continue with the teaching. The next Friday night he was
sitting right alongside me as I talked to the young people.
And instinctively, as one usually does, I just knew that he
was beginning to 'freeze'. The good-byes that evening lacked
their normal warmth, and I knew that Dennis was having a
considerable problem over this issue. I told Jill that night
that I thought that Dennis would probably tell me before
next Friday's meeting that he would be withdrawing his
young people from the partnership. I was away on the
Monday, and when I returned, Jill said to me, 'You were
right! Dennis and Shirley have asked if they can speak to us
on Wednesday evening, and I've promised them we will have
no other engagements'! Well, at least we knew that the
moment of decision had come!

As we sat in our lounge on that Wednesday evening, 23
July, 1981, I couldn't help but feel, as I quietly observed
Dennis, that he was going through all 'the hell' that I had
gone through during my first year in Mutare. He was greatly
agitated, and continually fidgeted with the Bible in his
hands. He was obviously having some difficulty in deciding
how to set about the discussion that lay ahead and suddenly,
almost as if he could no longer control the perplexity and
frustration and perhaps even anger within him, something
went snap and he almost banged his Bible down on the
occasional table alongside him and said 'John, I just cannot
go along with your teaching on the Holy Spirit!' For the next
twenty minutes or so I felt as if I was riding some rather
rough rapids as he poured out a great stream of statements
and questions that revealed all the 'doubts' that were almost
literally tearing him apart:

'I've had the distinct impression that, because I haven't experienced what you have, that you would say that I'm not a proper Christian.'

'Are you trying to tell me that I didn't receive the Holy Spirit when I gave my life to Christ?'

'Are you saying that I haven't been properly ordained into the ministry?'

'If it hasn't been the Holy Spirit inspiring my sermons up to now, then where do you think that inspiration has come from?'

'Why do you speak about the baptism of the Holy Spirit as if it was something "extra" that everyone needs? What was wrong with my baptism? Confirmation?'

'What do you think the leaders and members of the congregation would say if these young people started talking in tongues? And in church, during a service?'

'The Bible stresses that there needs to be "order" in the church; not everyone doing their own thing!'

'It's all very well having enthusiasm, excitement and hand-clapping or waving at a YP or a Sunday School – but certainly not in church!'

'I get the impression that all my experience of the Holy Spirit – in my life, in my ministry, in the church – are not, in your eyes, authentic because I don't speak in tongues, or that there is something wrong because I haven't had the same kind of emotional experience that some of you people have had.'

I knew where Dennis was, because I myself had been that way before. I knew the turmoil and doubt concerning my own ministry and the ministry of the Church, and my anger at them being, supposedly, brought into question. In the next three hours I was able to take Dennis step by step through the same process that I had been through. Of course he had the Holy Spirit in him, for no one can confess 'Jesus is Lord' unless the Holy Spirit enables him to do so. And if He enables you, then He also 'remains with you and is in you' (John 14:17) and will 'make you remember all that I have told you' (John 14:26), for it is 'the Spirit who reveals the truth' (John 15:26) – and 'leads you into all truth' (John 16:13). And at

times like his baptism, confirmation and ordination the Holy
Spirit *had* been at work. Perhaps the words 'Receive the Holy
Spirit' had been said over him, just as Jesus had said them to
the apostles on the evening of the day of the Resurrection –
and nothing had apparently happened. But we know that
Jesus did not *say* those words and give nothing with it! Jesus
would never do anything like that. I explained the difference,
as I saw it, between receiving the Holy Spirit as 'a Person',
and seeing the *power* of the Holy Spirit released in us.

I reminded him of all the occasions when people were filled
with the Holy Spirit in the Acts of the Apostles – and how
something always seemed to happen that was a confirmation
of that empowering. Samaria is, perhaps to some, a 'debat-
able case', and yet even here something happened that was so
startling that 'Simon *saw* that the Spirit had been given to the
believers . . .' and said, 'Give this power to me too . . .' (Acts
8:18–19). He saw something that spoke of power, and not
just 'hands laid on their heads'. In the home of Cornelius
'while Peter was still speaking, the Holy Spirit came down on
all those who were listening . . .' For they heard them
speaking in strange tongues and praising God's greatness
(Acts 10:44, 46) – just as had happened on the day of
Pentecost!

Even Paul, then, expected the Holy Spirit to come in such
a way that it would be remarked upon. Otherwise why would
he ask such a pointless question of 'the believers' he thought
he had found in Corinth – 'Did you receive the Holy Spirit
when you became believers?' And their answer was, 'We
have not even heard that there is a Holy Spirit.' Paul
discovered that they had only received John the Baptist's
baptism – so he prepared them, baptised them in the name of
Jesus, and then 'Paul placed his hands on them, and the Holy
Spirit came on them'. They soon realised that they had
received the Holy Spirit because immediately after Paul laid
hands on them, 'they spoke in strange tongues, and also
proclaimed God's message' (Acts 19:2–6).

Dennis was able to see how I understood the difference
between 'receiving the Person' of the Holy Spirit, and experiencing 'the release of his power' from within us. Both of
us had indeed gone as far as we were able – within the

limitations of what the Church had taught us. So, although
we had loved Jesus all through our lives, we had only been
able to 'give as much of ourselves as we could, to as much of
God as we were able to understand' at any given point in our
lives. What had happened to both of us – as it does, tragically
enough, to countless people within the Churches – was that
the Holy Spirit had remained dormant, asleep, within us.
And all because we had been taught *not* to expect anything
else. Because of that, we had never discovered the key that
would help us unlock the floodgates to a power-filled life.

The floodgates, I assured Dennis, was a good, expressive
word to use for it, because in St John's Gospel (7:37–39)
Jesus speaks about the streams of living water that will pour
out from our hearts. Did we want those floodgates to open?
'Whoever is thirsty,' said Jesus, 'should come to me and
drink. As the Scripture says, "Whoever believes in me,
streams of life-giving water will pour out from his heart."
Jesus said this about the Spirit, which those who believed in
Him were going to receive. At that time the Spirit had not yet
been given, because Jesus had not been raised to glory.'

How easy Jesus had made it for us to receive that power-
filled life through the Holy Spirit. I showed Dennis that
moving and descriptive passage in St Luke's Gospel where
Jesus had taught His disciples to pray the Lord's Prayer.
Jesus had gone on to tell a story of a man needing bread to
feed a visitor, and how he knocked-up a neighbour in the
middle of the night to try and obtain that bread. He ended
the story with these words: 'I tell you that even if he will not
get up and give you the bread because you are his friend, yet
he *will* get up and give you everything you need *because* you
are not ashamed to *keep on asking*. And so I say to you: Ask,
and you will receive, seek and you will find, knock and the
door will be opened to you.' And just as the father of a child,
says Jesus, will always give good things to a child – so 'much
more, then, will the Father in Heaven give the Holy Spirit to
those who ask him' (Luke 11:1–13).

I gave a graphic overview of my own early ministry and the
almost constant sense of failure that went with it. I also
pointed out how hurt I had been at what I 'thought' people
were saying of my ministry – or rather, lack of ministry – and

how I had discovered that, in most cases, it was quite untrue.

Instead of worrying about what anyone thought, I showed Dennis that my only concern, after recognising that I certainly had lacked the release of the Spirit in power, was that I should be willing and ready to accept anything God wanted to give me that would make my life and my ministry more effective for Him. I wanted those life-giving streams of water to well up and overflow my being. I saw how effective the ministry had been in New Testament times. If the Holy Spirit could do it for those men then, He could do it for us now, because God is the same yesterday, today and tomorrow. He does not change. And the state of the Church in New Testament times obviously bore no comparison to the Church of today with its present poverty, its millstone of an overbearing weight of nominal Christians, and its divisions and lack of love. And whatever the ridicule I would have to face in the Church of today, I wanted what they had – the 'baptism of the Spirit' as Jesus describes it in the first chapter of Acts. Perhaps, I said to Dennis, our mistake had been that we had not 'waited in Jerusalem' for the *release* of that power before we set out on our respective ministries. Jesus said, 'Do not leave Jerusalem, but wait for the gift I told you about . . .' for 'when the Holy Spirit comes upon you, you will be filled with POWER' (Acts 1:4, 5, 8).

I didn't know whether I was making any sense to Dennis and Shirley, they had both been quiet for so long. It was during a pause, while I tried to think of anything else that I might say to help them to understand, that they both surprised us by going down on their knees on the floor and saying: 'That's what we want. Please lay hands on us for the power of the Holy Spirit to be released in us.' Jill and I did so. Within moments tremendous joy and peace filled them both and Dennis was given a wonderful language to pray in. When I telephoned him after breakfast the next morning, he was still bubbling over with joy. He said that he had no desire for sleep when he had got home, and had prayed all night in his new tongue!

As you can imagine, our 'joint' ministry to the young people just seemed to 'take-off' after that. The next Saturday I completed the teaching on the baptism of the Holy Spirit, and quite a number of people were baptised and given a tongue to pray in. The next week, quite a few more followed. It was the week after that that a number of the young people who had conducted the youth mission came down to celebrate its anniversary with us. During the afternoon we all spent time worshipping the Lord in between braai-ing (barbecueing) our suppers. After supper we went over to our church hall and continued with another time of extended worship. It was a nice clear evening when we started.

During the course of the evening we thought a storm was getting up, for the wind seemed to be roaring all round the building. Suddenly, I noticed that the girl opposite me in the circle – Susan – seemed to be in an almost trance-like state, with her arms and hands raised above her head, and standing quite motionless. Her lips were moving and her eyes were closed. It went on for so long that some of the girls near her – who had never experienced the working of the Holy Spirit before – thought something was wrong with her and began to lead her to the outside door. By this time I had noticed that several others were in a similar state. I went across to Susan and realised as I reached her that she had in fact received the in-filling of the Spirit and was actually praising God in tongues. I explained to her friends what was happening, and we opened the doors to take her out. It was only then that we discovered that the noise was 'inside' the building – and that outside it was a completely clear, still night! The experience touched many lives. It was spoken of in the schools. Many mocked the believers, but from that day on there was a growing and steady stream of youngsters pouring through our house, sharing their lives and being counselled. Many lives were changed.

Our ministry to the young people of Mutare became a real focal-point during the next six years, enriching our own lives tremendously. Saturday evenings were looked forward to with much joy, anticipation and excitement, but our most important work amongst them was training them to minister in their own right. From the end of my first year in Mutare, my whole concept of what 'the ministry' was all about had changed radically. No longer was I to be the kingpin in the parish, responsible for most of the ministry. Instead, my

function, as I saw it, was to train others to do the ministry.
My role was simply to be 'an equipper'. As St Paul so aptly
describes it in his Epistle to the Ephesians, some were
appointed to be apostles, others to be prophets, some to be
evangelists, and yet others to be pastors and teachers. For
what purpose? Simply so that they might equip *all* God's
people for the work of the Church! Why? So that those who
have now been specially equipped could set about building
up the body of Christ! And the end result of all this? That we
will *all* come to a oneness in our faith, and a oneness in our
knowledge of the Son of God (Eph. 4:11–13).

The young were systematically taught to minister. Many
of them, especially our own children Andrew and Diana,
soon obtained guitars and taught themselves to play by ear.
In a truly miraculous way they were able to play dozens of
songs almost immediately. They were soon able to share
their testimonies of what God had done in their lives, and to
lead people to Christ, pray for them to be baptised in the
Holy Spirit, and pray for healing in a wide range of circumstances. What drew so many to the YP was the deep love,
care and concern these young people had for one another
right across the age-range, without any sign of the usual peer
groups developing. It was not that they wanted to be super-
spiritual at their YP meetings – but the games part of the
evening was soon crowded out because they were so hungry
for the word of God, and for their desire to meet the many
needs of the young people. It was not unusual to find our
home filled with young people almost every afternoon of the
week after school – quite often including a new person who
was looking for help in his or her life. Dennis was also a
frequent visitor. Regretfully, Dennis and Shirley were called
to a new congregation in South Africa just over two years
ago. We were very sad to see them move away.

But God's timing is always perfect even though we often
have the temerity to question it. Frequently it is only when
we look back on events that we are finally able to acknow-
ledge that God's timing was right! And so it proved in our
case. A matter of six weeks or so before we were 'exiled' from
our home by the mob, we had decided to bring our YP to an
agreed end and hand the few we had left to another leader.

Large numbers had belonged to the YP. Most of the YP members of the other congregation had emigrated by the time Dennis and Shirley left. After that large numbers from the Anglican part of the YP had left – and almost all at the same time. Many parents had become concerned over declining educational standards and moved their children elsewhere. We also had a very large contingent who had just finished their 'O' and 'A' level examinations. Because there were no higher places of learning in Mutare for them, they moved to colleges and universities elsewhere, or sought jobs in the capital city of Harare. Most of them found good YPs elsewhere, and many are playing leading roles in them today.

All of them were wonderfully provided for before we left town so unexpectedly. God *knew* in advance, and they weren't left high and dry!

ELEVEN

UNDERSTANDING THE NORMAL CHRISTIAN LIFE

It was soon after realising that I was indeed a 'son of God', as Colin Urquhart so vividly describes it in *When the Spirit Comes*, that I realised that I still had some unfinished business to complete. And that was the embarrassing book that my assistant priest, Leslie Crampton, had given me on the occasion of my induction as Rector of Mutare – *The Normal Christian Life* by Watchman Nee. Twice I had tried to read it. The gift, to my rather sensitive conscience, had conveyed the impression that I needed to discover what the 'normal' Christian life was all about. And the very fact that I had been unable to progress beyond the first page – because I was unable to understand what it was saying – was decidedly embarrassing after fourteen years in the ministry! I now knew that I had to get to grips with that book and master the subject matter once and for all!

So for the third and, I hoped, last time I retrieved the book from the bedside cupboard where it had stayed out of sight but certainly not out of mind. That would have been too much to expect after what it had done to my ego! I went over to the church to study it, undisturbed. I was determined that this time I would not give up until I had mastered the subject matter of the whole book, so away I went. Each time I found myself at a loss to understand some principle or paragraph, I would just stop and ask the Holy Spirit to give me under-standing. That always seemed to work miracles. It was almost as if God wanted all those new doors to be unlocked for me. With breaks for meals and sleep, I completed the book in two days. It was an exciting revelation for me. The

Scriptures were opened up in such a way that I 'saw' things in Scripture that I had never seen before. For the first time I really began to understand, with a great wealth of detail, what Christ's death on the Cross at Calvary had actually accomplished for *me*. For the first time I began to understand *how* that death had satisfied God's required justice, and *how* my sin was washed away as if it had never been. And how the working of the Holy Spirit in power can add a new dimension to the living out of the Christian life.

I wrote detailed notes on all the major themes running through the book during that marathon two-day exercise. I wrote them in simple language that I could understand, drawing diagrams where necessary to help me work out how all the various threads linked together to make up the whole. It was a tremendously exciting experience. Afterwards the notes were typed up, and many copies made by members of the congregation. This came about after hearing me speak so excitedly about it that they wanted to read the book for themselves. They used my notes to help them understand the theological arguments with great success! Surely it is just that kind of excitement that Paul is speaking of in the passage from Ephesians where he says: 'We shall all come together to that oneness in our faith and in our knowledge of the Son of God' (Eph. 4:13). There is something catching about a desire to learn when the fire of enthusiasm is sparked off within us.

And that is just what happened in Mutare. Whenever we came across something exciting in Scripture we brought it along to the next daily prayer time in the chapel, or to the next meeting if that came first! Sometimes we would not be able to wait, and so we shared it over the telephone with one another. In our own church we used a new South African lectionary that provided three readings a day from Scripture to cover every day of the year over a two-year cycle. Each day there would be a reading from the Old Testament, the New Testament (apart from the Gospels) and a lesson from one of the four Gospels. Psalms were also set for each day's use. It was surprising how much we learnt together after pooling what different people had 'seen' through the lessons and Psalms. Many new insights were given to us.

Another thing that happened was that we brought God

into almost everything. Our prayer lives took on a totally new dimension. Apart from praying together as a group at least each weekday there were also times of praying together in our homes in pairs. If ever anyone had a need – whether for self, a member of the family or group, for someone taken into hospital, or in danger of losing their life – we would be on the telephone to each other. Frequently, when unable to get together physically, praying was actually done while on the telephone to one another. And occasionally, a 'freak' took place (with three people wanting to contact one another) when 'one' would be dialling 'two', and 'three' dialling 'one', and all three telephones were linked together! An engineer told us it was just a matter of perfect timing!

Telephone 'chains' were soon established. The chains were used to pass round 'priority' and 'serious' prayer requests. The first person contacted the next two people on the list, and they in turn each contacted two people. We operated it in such a way that the prayer chains of all the denominations in Mutare were brought into operation simultaneously. Within a very short space of time we could have hundreds of people praying. And we learnt the truth of that statement 'more is wrought by prayer than this world dreams of'. During the war, which was now seriously escalating in our part of Zimbabwe, that linked prayer chain was constantly in operation and we heard of many wonderful answers to prayer.

All the farming community in our Manicaland Province – just as in many other provinces – were linked to a central control in Mutare through an Agric-Alert Radio system. It also included others in lonely outposts. It was manned twenty-four hours a day. Each day every station was called up morning and evening to find out if all was well, and important messages were radioed through. If any station didn't answer their call, a security force patrol would be despatched to check out the farm. When a station came under an attack from guerillas or 'freedom fighters' (those communist-backed revolutionary groups fighting for the overthrow of the Smith Government in Rhodesia prior to Independence in 1980), they were able to press the Agric-Alert button on their set and get instant access to control. If able to do so, they could then give a brief report of the size of the attack, and units would be despatched to bring help. If they were already under fire and unable to speak, the pressing of the button was enough for central control to be able to identify the call and send a fire-force to help them.

We had people serving on the control who were able to call up the head of the prayer chain, whatever hour of the day or night, and have dozens of people praying for God's protection during that particular attack while it was still in progress. I could give many instances where I believe the power of prayer worked, but I will only give one here. Our control had just received news of such an attack, and our prayer chains had alerted many people in Mutare to pray. It concerned two devoted Christian parents and their family who lived a hundred miles south of us near Chipinge, the first large municipal township to the south of Mutare. Theirs was a very isolated home, and particularly vulnerable because it was constructed of wood. A twenty-strong guerilla group had cut through the security fence late at night and approached to within twenty yards of the house. All the family were in the two front rooms that had large picture windows. The gang opened up with automatic weapons and rocket grenades. Two hundred and fifty rounds of armour-piercing bullets riddled the house, and two rocket grenades exploded against it but caused no injury. A third came through the window where Lynn Alexander (the wife) lay on the floor, but got entangled in the curtain above her head and failed to explode! Had it done so it would certainly have killed her. None of the family were hit by the automatic fire, which literally raked the building from one end to the other at hip height, because they were all lying on the floor. But the baby was still lying in the crib along that same wall at that height. Every bullet penetrated that outside wall and embedded itself in the wall on the other side of the room, or in objects within the room – except for three bullets which should have penetrated the cot. Only at that point, the bullets failed to penetrate the last half-inch of wood, and the baby survived unscathed! One of the attacking group then pulled the pin on a grenade – but accidentally(?) dropped it in the dark and couldn't find it. The blast that killed him made the gang think that Phil

Alexander, the husband, was now retaliating, and nineteen of them fled away through the fence. An army major, surveying the damage the next day, came to the conclusion that the family was only saved from death by God's intervention.

At a service the next Sunday in Chipinge, Phil shared a passage of Scripture as he testified to the great things that God had done. And it was this:

> I think you ought to know, dear brothers, about the hard time we went through in Asia. We were really crushed and overwhelmed, and feared we would never live through it. We felt we were doomed to die and saw how powerless we were to help ourselves; but that was good, for then we put everything into the hands of God, who alone could save us, for He can even raise the dead. And He did help us, and saved us from a terrible death; yes, and we expect Him to do it again and again. *But you must help us too, by praying for us.* For much thanks and praise will go to God from you who see his wonderful answers to your prayers for our safety (2 Cor. 1:8–11, The Living Bible).

We knew that 'call to prayer' was to remind us to continue steadfast in prayer, and it was *because* we saw so many miracles in answer to prayer, that prayer became so much a part of our lives. Each new miracle increased our faith in what God could and would do. Emergency calls to prayer were always responded to, whatever the hour of the day or night, with groups of people in each home praying perhaps at 3 a.m. for a family under attack. Quite often 'your' children would be praying for 'their' children, some of whom would be bosom pals at school. Apart from prayer for emergencies, there was on-going consistent prayer for every part of Manicaland. Each prayer group in Mutare was given a sector of the province to pray for, and would pray for every person on every farm and homestead – correspondence was often entered into between the parties so that they could pray for special needs, or fears.

The war gave a sense of urgency to everything we did. It was all too true that tomorrow we might be dead. People were dying almost every week in ambushes, exploding mines on the roads, attacks on farms and stores. Many would be personally known to us. Yet it was good when we saw that we were powerless to help ourselves, for then we did indeed – as Paul did – put everything into the hand of God. We lived 'in the valley of the shadow of death', but in no way were we despondent or cast down. Death was something we learned to live with. Nothing, however, could be more difficult than trying to minister to a family of unbelievers when a member of the family had been killed.

One of the things I came to dread was the ring of the telephone in the early hours of the morning, because it usually involved going down to army headquarters to be notified of someone's death, and then going to visit the family concerned to break the news to them. The clergy were always given this task. When it involved unbelievers or nominal Christians, it all too often consisted of a heart-rending scene, for they often railed against God. Sometimes they would find it impossible to accept that the loved one was dead, particularly when no recognisable body could be produced for identification; nor could they bring themselves to forgive the enemy, and so hatred would grow in them like a canker, with vengeance a foremost thought in their minds.

Where death happened amongst born-again Christian families who were certain of their place in God's Kingdom, there was a great contrast. Obviously the shock and the grief at their own loss was there, but there was also forgiveness for the enemy – which was in itself a means of healing. There was the assurance that separation from the loved one was only temporary. More than that, there was the desire not to grieve for, but to *rejoice* with, the departed loved one because he or she had now entered into the joy of the Lord for ever.

David Watson, in his book *Fear no Evil* (written while he was dying of cancer) describes the radical change that took place in his life at this time. It was a 'coming to terms' with death. He recognised that as a Christian his mental attitude had always been, 'I'm willing to die, Lord Jesus, but please – not yet!' He found that scripturally the right attitude should have been, 'Lord, I want to be with you NOW – but if you have something for me to do first, then I'm willing to wait behind and do that for you.'

St Paul describes it so perfectly. 'For what is life? To me, it is Christ. Death, then, will bring more. But if by continuing to live I can do more worthwhile work, then I am not sure which I should choose. I am pulled in two directions. *I want very much to leave this life and be with Christ, Christ is a far better thing*; but for your sake it is much better that I stay alive' (Phil. 1:21–24). That was the kind of transformation that was taking place in many of us as Christians. We just couldn't wait to be with the Lord – and almost envied those who were called home to be with Jesus prematurely before we were!

A remarkable case that sticks forever in my mind concerns a dear friend of the family, and member of our parish, Betty. She had been an orphan and grown up with loneliness, fear and deprivation very much to the fore in her life. When she married her husband, he did almost everything for her. When we first came to know her, she had been married for over twenty years, but knew nothing of her husband's business affairs, did not have a bank account, nor did she even know how to write a cheque. Nor had she ever felt confident of her ability to cope with such things. Not long after giving her life to the Lord, she came to one of our groups and expressed startled amazement that her husband Howard had begun to show her things 'she ought to know' about their business, and where to find all the important documents, contracts and other papers he had always handled in the past. He even taught her how to keep a bank account and how to write cheques! The question in her mind was, 'Why?'

In the very early hours of the morning I received one of those dreaded telephone calls. An army encampment had been mortared during the night and Howard had been killed. Would I please break the news to Betty? It must have been between 3 a.m. and 4 a.m. when I arrived at her door and tried to wake her up. As she came to the door, and opened it, she said, 'John, I know why you have come. Just tell me, is it my son, or is it Howard?' When I told her it was Howard, her very next comment was, 'All things work together for good to them that love God and are fitting into his purposes' (Rom. 8:28, Living Bible). During the next forty-eight hours before the military funeral, she shared with all those who visited her home how God had prepared her for this moment, even to the extent of her husband sharing with her everything she ought to know. The normal roles were reversed in that house of mourning. It was Betty who consoled the hundreds of people who poured through her house. It was her courage and steadfast faith in a loving God that were a real testimony to the whole community. And there were many others like her.

During those dark days, when most Rhodesians backed away from any suggestion of visiting our part of the country, the President made an unusual presentation to Mutare – the award of the MCM (Meritorious Conduct Medal) as a mark of honour from the rest of the country for the courage and determination of the people of Mutare and the whole province of Manicaland to survive through times of great danger. The citation went as follows:

> The people of the City of Umtali (Mutare) have stood in the front line in the struggle against the forces of barbarism and tyranny since the closure of the Mozambique border in March 1976. Their steadfastness, courage and fortitude in the face of perpetual danger from terrorist attacks both within and outside Rhodesia have been magnificent and deserving of the highest admiration.

This is the first and only time that such an award has been made to a community in Zimbabwe. It was awarded on 2 March, 1979. Mutare had already sustained several mortar and rocket attacks, both from positions just over the border, and from the hills overlooking the city and it would be another year before the senseless war was brought to an end. However, the verse from Scripture that Betty quoted on her husband's death, was one which was never far from our lips: 'All things' – yes!, even death, and destruction, and man's inhumanity to man – 'work together for good to them that love God and are fitting into his purposes.' Many of us thanked God for those days, in that it brought about a radical change in our relationship to God. From something half-hearted to something whole-hearted. Material possessions lost their importance, and the only reality was God and our present and future life with Him forever. That war situation changed our whole attitude to what the 'normal' Christian life so often ends up becoming in practice.

Colin was someone with whom I spent quite a bit of time, and a real sense of cameraderie developed between us. He was always saying that my sermons spoke of a kind of faith and trust that was beyond him. He had gone through very hard times with personal problems, the tragic death of a much loved son, the break-up of marriage and family and tremendous financial difficulties. His faith had undoubtedly grown tremendously over those years, and there was developing within him a real personal knowledge of Jesus. Just before I left Mutare – such a wrench for all of us – he brought me a copy of something that he had up on the wall of his office. I have no idea who the author is, but it expresses exactly what God did in our lives through those years:

WHAT JESUS COULD HAVE SAID TO ME

Do you really trust me?
If you do, why are you so afraid of the truth?
Have you forgotten that because I am Eternal
I am already in the future?
If you place your confidence in Me,
You will not be disappointed, for I will lead
You in My Way – and love, joy, peace and power
Will be with you and in you at all times.
Only you must trust Me, even in those moments
When you are not feeling particularly religious and
When cold human logic seems more sensible than
My Way of Faith. Trust Me when everything
You treasure seems to be threatened by circumstances
And conditions over which you have no control.
Trust Me in moments of loneliness when you seem
To stand without the support of your friends against
overwhelming odds.

(Author Unknown)

TWELVE

POWER OF GOD IN PREACHING

It must have been during the year after my experience of the baptism of the Holy Spirit that I began to be challenged in the area of preaching. For the previous eighteen months in particular, I had put a lot of work into the sermons that I prepared. Although I didn't write them out word for word, a large part of the content of what I would preach was down in written form so that I wouldn't 'get lost' in moving from one point to another. I still did not feel comfortable about my sermons, and began to spend more and more time 'waiting on the Lord' for inspiration and help. Nevertheless, a sense of unhappiness after a sermon, perhaps because of the lack of response from the congregation, or the wrong response – 'I really enjoyed your sermon this morning'! – persisted. Had I only given pleasure and entertainment?

The good thing about the Lectionary (list of readings) that we used was that it gave a theme for each of the hundred and four Sundays and special feast days over a two-year period. And for each theme there was an excellent selection of three readings from Old and New Testaments and one of the Gospels. Sometimes it was quite interesting trying to discover the threads that ran through all three. It was also a challenge to the preacher that one or two groups in the parish used the set of lessons for their Bible Study in the week before they would be used in church on Sunday. Some of them would be quite disappointed if you didn't pick up and mention what they had discovered! It wasn't unusual, in that case, to be pulled up short outside church after the service, and told that you had missed the most important, or the most interesting, point.

Of course it was tremendous having people in the congregation undertaking that kind of study, and they obviously drew far more out of the lessons and sermon than the average person who came virtually unprepared! And at our house churches – when a group that normally met for Bible Study and Fellowship would meet once in a while for 'breaking of bread' in the home – three different people would be asked to read the three lessons set for the day and give a brief 'sermon' (after each lesson) on what was meaningful and significant to each of them. Then there would be an opportunity for anyone else to share what they heard the lesson saying to them. This developed even further, with a number of lay people preaching at Sunday evening services. Interest in the preached word was growing. We had a good many who were listening for what they believed God was saying to them through preaching.

I increasingly felt convinced that I wasn't really saying what *God* wanted me to say. I could read the lessons and read up what many great authorities thought about each of the lessons, and produce sermons that would be acceptable to my theological college lecturers! What I really wanted to see was people convicted of sin, people challenged out of their 'hobby' of going to church and to see them making a radical commitment of their lives to Christ. Although I didn't expect to get the results that Peter got after his first sermon, when 3,000 were saved, I longed for the day when people would be regularly saved through hearing the preaching of the Word of God.

It was a year or two later at another clerical retreat (five blissful days of silence) that God spoke to me about this area of my ministry. It was on about the third day when I actually believe God 'spoke' to me because the message was so clear: 'You don't trust me!' That really brought me up short. Of course I trusted Him. My whole life had radically changed in the past few years. I trusted Him with my very life on almost every journey I went on. I trusted Him to protect my family through war. I trusted Him that my salvation was assured. So what did He mean when He said I didn't trust Him? It very soon dawned on me what it was. I didn't trust Him to provide the words for my sermon. Instead, with lots of preparation and study – nothing wrong in that – I wrote down all the main points of what I would say. It reminded me of the little girl who asked her mother what father was doing in his study. On being told that he was writing down what God wanted him to say in the pulpit on Sunday, the little girl said to her mother, 'Then why does he have so many crossings out!' Many can write polished and erudite sermons that will win the applause of men. They may be well sand-wiched, with superb illustrations and apposite quotations from great men over the ages, but do they change lives? Even more important, are they really the words that God would have on our lips, or are we just out to please our hearers? It is interesting, isn't it, that Peter's words to the crowd at Pentecost were not the most eloquent but they were words that (i) came from the heart, (ii) spoke of the apostle's *personal experience*, (iii) charged the crowds with responsibility for Jesus' death(!) and (iv) challenged them to change their lives. Above all else, the bulk of what he said came direct from the Word of God in Scripture. The only response that sermon elicited from that crowd was a cry from their hearts, 'Brothers, what must we do to be saved?'

I knew I was back facing the challenge that Pam Braatvedt had given me all those years before. Yet how could I possibly go into the pulpit without having mapped out, in advance, all that I was going to say. Wouldn't I just be a laughing stock when nothing was forthcoming and I would have to say to the congregation: 'Sorry! I don't seem to have anything for you today!' I couldn't ignore the fact that the rest of that retreat seemed to be leading me in that direction. Was I prepared to trust God to provide for me when the time came? With the largest batch of stomach 'butterflies' I think I have ever had, I left that retreat with a determination to do just that – trust God to provide the words that I would need on Sunday morning. I also knew that there would be a further price to pay – the need to spend the whole of Saturday night in prayer and in waiting on God.

Saturday evening arrived and all went well until about 2 a.m. Then I said to God that I was just going to read through the lessons for the morning. Immediately came the response, 'You don't trust me, do you?' With a certain amount of misery I gave in, continued in prayer and in listening to God. About an hour before I was to go and get ready to take the service, I thought that at last I could now look up the theme for the day and quickly glance through the set lessons. Again came that challenge, 'You still don't trust me, do you?!' I remained obedient and kept the books closed, but when I started that service, I felt like a lump of lead. After the hymn and opening prayers, the Old Testament and New Testament lessons were read by people from the congregation. Then we had another hymn. I still couldn't piece together a theme because I hadn't read the Gospel lesson for the day. Up into the pulpit I went – more unwillingly than any schoolboy trudging off to school, but grateful once more for the high wooden sides that hid my shaking legs! I called out the page and reference for the Gospel and read it. The moment had arrived – the sermon! I hadn't a thought in my mind! Lord, I am now trusting you – so over to you! I remember little about that sermon, and have often wished that I had recorded it. One thing I *do* know is that I believed everything in that sermon was directed at me, with God challenging me in almost every area of my life. I do remember thinking at one stage that it was perhaps a little unfair of God to use the sermon-time to talk about *my* life – instead of a sermon that would have helped the whole congregation! Yet all through that sermon I noticed that the cold terror that had flooded my being rapidly drained away and I was filled with a tremendous warmth.

Despite those areas in which I was being convicted, I had a joyful knowledge of God's love and concern for me. As I stepped down from the pulpit to continue the service, I was surprised to see that I had preached for nearly thirty minutes – without a note!

It was after the service that I was really brought up sharp, for one person after another left the church visibly moved, and several had tears in their eyes. Some asked how I could 'possibly know that about me – you have been such an answer to prayer for me'. Almost everyone said something that revealed that they thought I was looking *only* at them during the sermon, and that I had touched on things they didn't think anyone knew about them. All I could do was to go back to the chapel, praising and thanking God that I could indeed trust Him. Despite the experience of this Sunday, I knew it was NOT God's intention that I stop studying the Scriptures for each Sunday, or just go 'empty' into the pulpit, but He showed me a new way which I have used ever since. If the words of my parishioners in my last year in Mutare are to be believed, the sermons have had a greater and more telling effect as time has gone by.

The Lord showed me after that Sunday service that in future – some time after the Sunday services and before going to bed – I should read through, and mull over, all three lessons for the following Sunday. I would also try and understand the connection with the theme in each of the lessons, and of any other themes I noticed. Then I would 'put it all to bed' in my mind and heart for the rest of the week. On the Monday or Tuesday I would look up a wide spectrum of commentaries on the texts – from traditional Anglican through Evangelical to Pentecostal oriented ones. (One begins to gather very interesting insights when one studies a passage looked at from the different angles and perspectives of scholars from such varied churchmanship.) All through the week the material would be kept in mind, often sub-consciously, with the themes being related to the events and situations of the week, and to their relevance and effec-tiveness for family, church, community and country. Ideas that came to mind would be committed to prayer, not paper.

By Saturday evening I would usually have a picture of the main thrust for the sermon, and of the Scriptures that would be underlined to draw out the relevance of that thrust to God's word and our daily situations. I would always end the evening by reading through the lessons for a final time before going to sleep. As a result the readings were subconsciously running through my head as I slept. Many is the time when I have been woken up at 2 or 3 in the morning with either a totally new angle on those Scriptures that I had not seen before, or with a crystal clear illustration from real life that would vividly bring to life what I believed God was wanting to say to us through those Scriptures. However good my material seemed to be, I never wrote it down, for I still knew that I had to go into that pulpit on a Sunday morning with an open mind.

Sometimes it was only while I was actually reading the Gospel – or listening to the other two readings – that a verse or a word would almost seem to light-up like a neon sign, and the whole direction and thrust of the sermon that had been in preparation in my mind all week would be radically altered.

It was still an uncanny feeling to have to put away – at the last minute – what one had thought of using, but I began to experience a real excitement within me whenever it happened – as with the sermon on the day the Cathedral was invaded by that rampaging mob! And there was a joy and a delight in somehow knowing that this was of God, and not me, because I had never had the natural ability or confidence to speak like that.

Something seemingly insignificant at first, which led to a tremendous growth in my faith and consequent confidence in preaching, was the knowledge that God had been there before. I need to explain what I mean by that statement. During those war years, (and subsequently) we had many 'special' services. National Days of Prayer for an end to war, for 'solutions' acceptable to the warring factions; for thanksgivings for various deliverances from mortar attacks and the like; and even things like national or community days to pray for rain during a crippling drought. Never once for any of those special events did I ever have to search for an appropriate selection of readings for the occasion. We never once changed the ordinary lessons that were already set down for that particular date in our church Lectionary. The lessons for each day over a recurring two-year cycle had been drawn up some years before. When thinking of Lectionaries and how they come into being, one sometimes has a vision of boffins sitting with damp towels around their heads, trying to put together an orderly pattern of lessons that will take account of the church's year, the set pattern of feasts, and the need to read systematically through all the books of the Bible. Yet those boffins could not, by any stretch of the imagination, know that in three, or five, or eight years' time, there would be a special service for this or that in Mutare, or in Zimbabwe!

Yet for every special service we ever had (and remember that in most cases we had nothing to do with choosing the day) the lessons set down in our Lectionary for that very day were the most appropriate – and usually the most devastatingly pertinent – that one could hope to find. And at every one of these services, I used the sermon to draw attention to this fact. After a while, people began to sit up and take notice. We were dealing with a God to whom nothing was impossible. God *knows* the end from the beginning. He had been there before us – and years before, without their realising it, inspiration and direction had been given to those compilers to select exactly what was right for 'that' day for us in our situation!

My own ministry in preaching has moved away from a kind of distant, impersonal and rather theoretical preaching of the Gospel to a more personalised sharing of myself and God's day-to-day dealings with us as a body seen through Scripture. Some of St Paul's words have meant a great deal to me in recent years: 'I can be proud of my service for God. I will be bold and *speak ONLY about what Christ has done through me* to lead the Gentiles to obey God. He has done this by means of words and deeds, by the power of miracles and wonders, and by the power of the Spirit of God', (Rom. 15:17b–19a).

I was led to be more and more open in baring my own soul before my congregation. The more honest I was in sharing my fears, failings and lack of knowledge – and the great things that God was doing to rectify these things in my life – the more the congregation was able to identify with me and be encouraged in their own struggles. I spoke frequently of actual miracles that had taken place in the lives of individuals in the congregation during the previous week, which brought many to an understanding that God was indeed very much alive and active in our midst. They would sometimes return home from the service with 'goosepimples running up and down the middle of their backs'. That was how real God was to us! And still is!

THIRTEEN

POWER OF GOD IN WARFARE

Terrorism and guerilla warfare in the twentieth century will go down in history as one of the most brutal, cowardly and sadistic forms of warfare, in which disproportionately small numbers have been able to hold virtually whole nations to ransom. Tiny groups of men and women – for the most part indistinguishable from the rest of the people – can render nations virtually powerless because 'the enemy' adopts cowardly hit and run attacks on soft targets, lays landmines without any concern as to who will be blown up, and terrorises the population because it never knows where the unseen 'enemy' will attack next. This warfare is worse than any plague in history and has Africa, in particular, by the jugular; and it is slowly destroying it. It has been used by one nation after another to obtain its freedom.

Neither side is ever 'holier than thou' – the uncontrollable and more sadistic element on either side going to any barbarous lengths to achieve their ends, or ostensibly 'pay back' the other side for what they have done to them. Those who have won 'freedom' for their people have regrettably, all too often, 'sanctified' a vicious and evil form of warfare that is now used by black opponents to oust former liberators *ad infinitum*. The black leaders now in power are appalled that their own countrymen should use the tactics of guerilla warfare against them, and brand it as 'barbaric' and 'unacceptable' to mankind, and its perpetrators as 'murderers' who must be brought to justice. Africa is over-run by a neverending, and bloody, tug-of-war for final supremacy. This is the case in Ethiopia, Uganda, Zaire, Angola and Mozambique, where a very small but vociferous group, has got into power and civil war has continued unabated ever since. The war in Zimbabwe (Rhodesia at that time) has brought much the same results. The whites entering Rhodesia ninety years ago brought to an end a seemingly ceaseless war. The warlike Matabele plundered, pillaged and decimated the Shona people at will. The latter lived in perpetual fear of these marauders. Seventy years later, these two 'nations' joined forces to win their 'freedom' from the whites, although for the most part under separate commanders – Robert Mugabe and Joshua Nkomo. Today, the 'shoe is on the other foot'. The Shona are in power and the Ndebele people a tiny minority.

Some of the Ndebele people who are dissatisfied at their relegation to a state of powerlessness in the new Zimbabwe – funded, some say, by a South African nation bent on destabilising the region – are now carrying out a guerilla war against the Shona party in power. The largest standing army in Zimbabwe's (or Rhodesia's) history is now stretched to its limits in facing a three-fold threat. It is trying to contain and capture the small bands that roam at will bringing death and destruction to 'soft' targets. Secondly, the country is being 'bled dry' trying to maintain that army – not only against those guerillas – but also in building up mammoth armaments against possible attacks from a really powerful South African army and thirdly, in the enormous defensive war being undertaken in Mozambique to guard Zimbabwe's 160-mile railway and oil pipeline 'corridor' through Mozambique to the sea at Beira. In this latter area, large parts of Mozambique are now no longer effectively controlled by the late Samora Machel's FRELIMO (communist) government, but are ravaged by the guerilla MRN movement.

There is no doubt whatever that Ian Smith's Unilateral Declaration of Independence on 11 November, 1965 was the final act of 'throwing down the gauntlet' to the African Nationalists. Ian Smith's 'no African rule in a thousand years' or 'in my lifetime' only added more fuel to the fire of determination to win independence from white domination at any cost. As with any guerilla war, terrible deeds were committed by both sides. Innocent villagers were interro-

gated and tortured – many of them suffering at the hands of
both sides – if interrogators thought that the villagers had
aided or abetted the 'other' side.

It was not surprising that many villagers were embittered.
All too frequently when a guerilla group met up with a
security force patrol, a group of villagers would be in between
and would take the main brunt of the vicious crossfire. It was
only after the war that we, as whites, came to understand
how much we had been brainwashed by 'propaganda material' through the government-controlled media. Partly as a
result of that, hostilities continued for over ten weary years
before Independence came to Zimbabwe.

In some ways it was scarcely a war at all. At no time did the
guerillas use tactics which could have totally paralysed the
country, although apparently having the manpower and
explosives to bring that about. Relationships between the
vast majority of whites and blacks in the towns, on the
surface at any rate, continued as normal. Many black and
white groups prayed together all through the war for a
solution to be found and for an end to the conflict. We prayed
with many blacks who were devastated when their children
were abducted (or voluntarily went?) over the borders to
fight with the 'freedom fighters'. We prayed for their safety
and for God's protection over them. In the country the most
obvious change was that the guerillas brought about the
closure or destruction of large numbers of schools, churches,
hospitals and clinics – and the determined efforts of the
'freedom fighters' were used to stop all government programmes in the Tribal Trust Lands – whether it be birth-
control, health, education or correct agricultural practices
(dipping to prevent tick infestation, land measures to prevent
soil erosion, etc.). Again, it was the villagers in those rural
communities who suffered the most. Almost all church life
stopped in many areas, with people being forced to close up
or destroy their churches, to burn their Christian literature,
including any Bibles, prayer books or hymn books, and being
'persuaded' to stop all church services and to go back to the
'ancestral worship' of their forebears.

In many ways it was probably the best thing that could
happen to the Church – particularly the Anglican Church.

We were over-burdened with a large number of nominal Christians. Many became members of a Church if it would enable them to enter the next stage of schooling in a local church school. Far too many 'members' were churchgoers when it suited them, but had no inhibitions or scruples about consulting the local witchdoctor when that was deemed necessary. In a small research project which I undertook just prior to the war really getting a grip on the country – and which shook my bishop to the core – I discovered that our Easter communicant level stayed virtually static at about 28,000, despite the bishop confirming as many as 6,000 new communicant members each year, over a period of nearly ten years! Large numbers of these nominal Church people quickly fell away during the war. It was largely the truly committed who remained faithful through the 'persecution'. God is still dealing with a number who have remained for one reason or another, but who still have reason to consult the witchdoctor and their 'ancestral spirits' on all important family matters. Fortunately, much of the top leadership of the Church has made a strong stand on this issue, and shown up those things that are incompatible with Christianity. Bishops Peter Hatendi and Elijah Masuko, amongst the black bishops of Central Africa, have been particularly courageous in speaking up against ancestral worship.

The very first mortar attack on Mutare took place in 1976 in the early hours of the morning, and the residents of the suburb of Greenside took the brunt of that attack which came from Machipanda, just over the border in Mozambique. Despite a large number of mortars being fired no one, quite miraculously, was killed. One person had a slight stomach wound from a 'splinter' after a mortar hit a heavy fencing post. Our son Andrew, about eleven at the time, was probably the only person in Mutare to sleep right through the whole attack! Another attack on Mutare that came from Machipanda involved a whole series of rockets just after 5 p.m. one Wednesday afternoon. It was early closing day, so most businesses had closed at 4 p.m. and the business centre was virtually empty. We later discovered that the prime target was the central police station – because as soon as an alert sounded, every able-bodied man in the city, serving in the police reserve, would report to that building for duty. One direct hit on that building could have killed, wounded or immobilised a large part of the city's defence manpower. Our leaders learnt quickly from that, and from then on had the men meet at several different points!

On this occasion, all the rockets came from the same rocket launcher, and all of them followed the same straight line. The first landed in a stream, the second in one of the senior girls' playing fields, and so on. Another one – from its trajectory and line of flight – should have gone right into the tallest high-rise block of flats (narrowly missing Central Police Headquarters) curved 'round' the building and landed in the road beyond, a few yards from a petrol station and about a hundred yards from both our house and the police station. It ploughed deep into the pavement between a number of stationary cars containing a number of garage employees' wives! (Garages did not observe early closing days and closed at 5.30 p.m.) This was the only rocket that failed to explode! The next day, it took the bomb squad eight hours to gingerly dig it out, and take it elsewhere to be detonated.

At the time of that rocket attack, I was about to conduct the blessing of a civil marriage, and a number of Christian friends had come round to lend support. Our garden was filled with 'our' small children, aged from three to fifteen. They had been so well trained in school as to what to do in the event of an attack, that as soon as they heard the first rocket, without any panic at all, they lined up 'crocodile' fashion and the older children led them all into our basement. It took us a little longer, in the church, to realise what was actually happening; when I ran out into the garden, the children were already safe! Soon all of us were in church singing God's praises and thanking Him for His protection. In no time several coloured families and quite a large number of black employees from neighbouring properties arrived in a state of shock – no doubt drawn by the singing – and asked to join us. A wonderful spirit of family fellowship developed as we prayed for release from fear, and our young children filled the place with their songs of praise. The couple who wanted their marriage 'blessed' never did turn up!

A T-shirt was produced after another rocket attack – this attack coming from the mountain to the north of (and overlooking) the city – with a slogan printed on it inviting people to come to Mutare because its golf courses had more 'bunkers' than any other golf course in the country! This attack took place just before a major national golf championship in Mutare. Although those firing the mortars had a perfect view of the whole city laid out below them in the valley, most of the mortars landed, instead, all over the golf course. Special rules were introduced for that tournament – because there had not been time to deal with the 'unapproved' bunkers – for golfers to take their golfballs out of 'these' bunkers without being penalised. Again no one was hurt in this mortar attack, although school boarding hostels and the hospital itself survived near misses.

One of the special blessings of the Agric-Alert system, which I have already mentioned, was that farmers were given a commentary on what was going on in Mutare, and parents were quickly given assurance that their children in the boarding hostels were safe. It can be imagined what untold agony this saved when farmers twenty and thirty miles away were woken by the explosions and knew they were coming from the direction of Mutare. The residents of Mutare were also helped by the security forces. The latter took over the local waveband on the radio as soon as an attack started and we were then given a running commentary on all that was taking place. Through every attack, each household moved into a safe area in the house. We used to make tea, serve biscuits, and have a time of prayer for the city's protection – while listening to the radio as it gave us up to the minute information.

After the very first mortar attack on Mutare, a large battery of guns was bedded-down in a valley just the other side of a range of hills to the south. In the event of further attacks from Machipanda in Mozambique, they could 'neutralise' that very quickly. And so it proved after the rocket attack on the police station. Machipanda was quickly 'knocked out'. When the next mortar attack came from the hills to the north of the city, the security chiefs decided that those guns to the south should also protect our northern flank. This entailed turning the guns around and shooting over the hills just south of the city, right across the valley in which the whole city was spread out, and 'homing in' on the top of the range north of us. This had to be very accurate, because if too short, the shells would hit the houses on the southern flank of that range, and if too long, would go over the range and hit the township on the other side! So they decided it would be important to have some target practice. The city was warned that on a certain afternoon, at 4 p.m., there would be a few ranging shots. Right on four, the first shot screamed over the city and landed right on top of the hill. Seconds later, there was the most appalling explosion right in the centre of the city. The guerillas had also learnt of the exercise and arranged for a bomb to be placed in the city timed to go off at 4 p.m. They had even gone one better. They informed the *Star* newspaper in Johannesburg – seconds before the event – that a bomb was about to go off in the Main Street of Mutare. While one of the *Star* reporters was on the telephone asking our *Manica Post* if they knew anything about it (and the local editor was telling the *Star* that only a military bombing practice was taking place) the bomb went off, shaking the whole city's morale. It was some time before we learnt that it was a bomb, and not a 'short shot from one of our guns', that caused the explosion! Bombs in shops were a nerve-racking experience for several years, and it was thanks to the tight security and the indignity of personal body searches and the searching of bags over a period of years, that we only suffered two major bomb explosions in Mutare – the sole casualty being the women who carried the one bomb into Meikles department store, where it went off prematurely.

It was quite a remarkable fact that during the many mortar attacks on Mutare, considering the compact nature of the city in a bowl surrounded by hills, that the city suffered no fatalities, and very few injuries. It was a reminder of something that many of us had seen just before one of these attacks. Nearly seventy of us had been away for a long weekend of 'renewal'. We had taken over a hotel up in the Nyanga Mountains. It was a very moving weekend for all of us. On the drive down to Mutare quite a large number of people, travelling in a number of different cars, all saw the same phenomenon. Just a single cloud, in the form of an enormous hand, seemingly placed directly over Mutare. All were given an absolute assurance that it was God's protection over our city. We carried that picture with us all through the guerilla war, and praised God that despite our unworthiness and many failures in bringing about a just solution to the war, His hand was over us, assuring us of His love, His care and His protection.

One night an army vehicle arrived at the Mutare Hospital with quite a number of wounded men. They had survived an ambush on the tar road just south of Mutare and the driver, realising how seriously hurt some of the men were, drove straight to the hospital. It was only after the wounded had been attended to – and the driver was climbing back into the cab of his vehicle – that he noticed an unexploded rocket precariously lodged in the bodywork of the cab immediately behind where he had been sitting. With all the subsequent jolting – in bringing in the vehicle from the point of ambush – it was a miracle the rocket never exploded. The driver literally turned as white as a sheet when he realised how close to death he had been, and gave thanks to God for their miraculous escape.

Armed convoys used to escort vehicles from one part of the country to another and became a regular part of our way of life. Major convoy routes covered the two main roads south from i) Harare via Masvingo to Beit Bridge on the South African border; and ii) from Bulawayo south to Beit Bridge.

A further major convoy route was established at a later stage on the road south from Mutare, through Birchenough Bridge, to Masvingo to join the main convoy route from Harare to Beit Bridge. Other convoy routes operated south of Mutare to two large centres, at Chipinge and Chimanimani – with a separate one to Cashel – and joined or left the main convoys from Mutare to and from Masvingo – and sometimes they set up their own armed convoys. Only one or two convoys a day ran on most of these routes and the majority of these roads were recommended no-go areas to the general public at other times. Convoys were usually protected by Landrovers armed with Browning machine guns mounted on a central swivel in the back of the Landrover – with a rudimentary seat attached so that the gunner could swing, with his gun, round a 360 degree radius. For the most part none of these gunners had any protection from enemy fire. Many had miraculous escapes during ambushes. Max Shepherd, a member of our congregation, was one of the police reservists manning such vehicles. In one ambush he was subjected to a hail of bullets from both sides of the road and not only survived totally unscathed, but was able to drive them off with his return fire. On rough roads, the gunner's position was precarious indeed – with only a strap round him and the central mounting to prevent him falling off – and with the vehicle bucking up and down and rocking from side to side at high speed, it was incredible that they could shoot at all when the unexpected attack came. In cold weather, they nearly froze to death because they had no protection from the elements. No fun being driven at 60 mph in such conditions.

On one occasion we were travelling back from a conference in South Africa, and our truck/caravan combination was too slow for the convoy. We were detached by the convoy commander (whose word was law, and who had to consider the safety of the greatest number) at the Bubye River, and had to travel the next 160 mile stretch on our own. It is quite an eerie experience when you have three hours to worry about the safety of your family. Once again, after Masvingo, we found we had to travel the next 195 miles without convoy protection for the same reason. We were considerably relieved to reach home in one piece. One Christian woman who greatly endeared herself to all of Mutare by her tremendous courage, determination and radiant cheerfulness was Ceylonia Joubert, whose vehicle had been blown practically to smithereens by a boosted landmine. For week after week, she lay in our hospital severely crippled and in great pain, not knowing for sure if she would ever be able to walk again. All of us as pastors used her at one time or another to speak to other patients who were often better off than she was, but who were distraught or who had lost hope for one reason or another. Ceylonia had a real Florence Nightingale ministry in that hospital. Praise God she finally walked again. She was one of the very last people I saw before leaving Zimbabwe in

1986 – still having to struggle to walk with any degree of ease, and always with pain – but still as cheerful as ever. Her story speaks of the courage of so many country folk during those days.

Another teenager was not so lucky. In another landmine incident, in the same area, she was made a quadraplegic for life. Two of our national airline planes were shot down with ground to air missiles while taking off from Kariba, a holiday resort, filled with tourists. The first crashed with the loss of everyone on board. In the second the pilot, in a quite outstanding feat, got the plane down practically in one piece in bush country. As many of the passengers thanked God for a truly miraculous escape, a group of terrorists arrived on the scene and massacred all those whom they found alive. Such barbarity defies explanation. Only those who had gone to seek help survived.

Of course, in all probability no two groups of guerillas were the same. One of our friends who lived in the Cashel area had just brought his children back to school at the beginning of a new term. Their youngest daughter was too young for boarding school and lived with us since Sarah and Diana were in the same class at school. Sue, the wife, went on to Harare to collect their 'new' second-hand car while Tim returned to Cashel. Before reaching home, he stopped to chat to the local MP, Des, who was inspecting his own lands. They spent some time chatting, and it was almost dark when they realised they must get home. Tim was the first to drive off and, at the first bend in the road, ran into a hail of bullets from an ambush. He tried to return the fire with his FN, only to find that practically the first bullet must have hit his weapon and jammed it. Lying there with serious wounds mainly in the area of his buttocks, he realised that this was probably the end. At any moment someone would come up and finish him off. But Des, with incredible courage, grabbed his FN from his vehicle and ran up the road, firing at Tim's attackers (I can't remember the exact number now, but there were about six of them). When he ran out of ammunition, he ran back to his vehicle to reload and return. By now, the guerillas had run off.

Tim was rushed into Mutare Hospital where, for a while, it

was thought that all would be well. Later on, though, they decided that they might be able to provide better facilities in Harare, and they put him on a plane to fly him up there. It was a terrible shock to hear that he died in the plane en route to Harare. Sue, with quite incredible courage, returned to the farm and kept it operating! But the most extraordinary event happened soon afterwards when she actually received a letter of apology from the guerilla group saying that they had never had any intention of hurting Tim. They thought that the first vehicle to have driven off was Des' vehicle, and it was him – as one of Ian Smith's MPs – that they were intent on killing. A very strange war indeed. It was also to affect Diana. To see Sarah's Daddy die as a result of that ambush really put a terrible fear in her heart every time I drove out of town. She would weep every time I went away, wondering if it would be the last time she would see me. She was only seven.

FOURTEEN

POWER OF GOD IN SEEMING TRAGEDY

Probably the most horrific and barbaric of all the atrocities committed in the war – and there were many – affected our community in Manicaland most of all. It concerned the Elim Pentecostal Church and their missionaries. They had run a large mission station to the north of Nyanga – very remote – for a good many years. During the war, with their roads being continually mined and since many threats were being made against them, they decided to take over an abandoned school in the Vumba Mountains on the southern edge of Mutare. Although continually urged to do so by the security forces, they refused to carry arms for their own protection. Late one night, a guerilla group moved into the school and, apparently without any of the black pupils being aware of what was happening, gathered together all the white missionaries – men, women, children and a babe-in-arms – took them out into the darkness on a bitterly cold winter's night, and cold-bloodedly butchered them to death with axes on the edge of the mountain side.

Only one woman survived the brutal attack that night, and crawled away into some bushes more dead than alive. She was not discovered at first the next morning, but when she was she was unconscious. She died some days later in hospital. Nothing was more harrowing than the mass funeral which followed in the Queen's Hall in Mutare. The pastors were asked to carry the coffins, and I carried the casket of the smallest baby. The only people of that Elim group to escape the massacre were the pastor/headmaster and his wife, Peter and Brenda 'G', who were away in England on furlough at the time and the children, of those butchered to death, who were away at boarding school. These children were flown home to relatives in England.

Twelve people died a martyr's death that night. A plaque has been erected in the Vumba Mountains overlooking that hillside with words that read something like this: 'Father, we do not understand! But we trust you.'

The words on the plaque were written by Mother Basilea of the Darmstadt Sisters in Germany. For the Christians, a note of victory ran through that funeral service, for we knew that the blood of martyrs is something very precious to God, and that it is never spilled in vain. The first 'miracle' that came out of the massacre was the result of the school being closed down. There were many strong 'born-again' and 'spirit-filled' Christians amongst the pupils of that school. They were divided up and fed into other schools where, in some cases, their Christian witness had a remarkable effect on improving the Christian witness amongst pupils who were only nominally Christian.

But how does one ever forgive the callous and brutal murderers? We knew at the funeral that we had to pray for their forgiveness, and for their salvation. Jesus could forgive His murderers while hanging on the Cross. We had to do likewise.

Peter, leader of the Elim Mission in Zimbabwe at the time of the massacre, was on furlough in England but he flew out for the mass funeral. Later, on his return to Zimbabwe, he heard of many persistent rumours circulating about the gang that had committed the crime. As he said, there is a need for Christians to beware of sensational rumours: 'the Bible teaches us, and it's a command laid upon us, "to prove all things" and then to "hold on to that which is good".' The Elim Mission Director in England, Brian Edwards, had also heard these rumours, and he asked Peter to investigate them. 'And very reluctantly I did,' says Peter.

He heard that the leader of the gang was training for the ministry at a Pentecostal bible college in Harare, Zimbabwe. The Canadian principal of the college was a friend of Peter's. When Peter asked Glen the truth concerning 'this man' at the college, Glen invited Peter to come and speak to the college, meet with this former guerilla afterwards – and then make his own assessment. After speaking to the college Peter was left in the principal's office with the man responsible for the killing of all his former colleagues and members of their families. Gavin, about twenty-eight years of age, told his story to Peter.

In 1974 he had been senior student of the top African secondary school in Zimbabwe, but he ran away and made his way north through the bush, and across the Zambezi, into Zambia to join the liberation struggle and be trained as an insurgent. This very bright lad was quickly singled out for his intelligence and leadership, and spent six months training as a political commissar. Then he was appointed as a platoon leader with sixteen other men. After re-entering Zimbabwe, this time from Mozambique, he found himself, in June 1978, operating in the Vumba area south of Mutare, and close to the Elim School. He decided to close down the school and kill the missionaries. There were a number of reasons for this, and these included: i) his desire to lower white morale in the country, and ii) by closing down all possible institutions in the area, to create a more effective infiltration route for other groups entering the country from Mozambique.

A message was sent to the missionaries to leave. This was relayed to the Mission Board in England and it was agreed that steps should be taken that would enable the missionaries to leave the area during hours of darkness. But only a matter of days after receiving the death threat, the gang moved into the school on the night of 23 June, 1978, because the missionaries had not acted with the swiftness that was required. The only point at which Peter interrupted the story was as Gavin began to describe what happened as they led the men, women and children out to their deaths. Peter asked, 'What did the missionaries do when they knew they were going to die?'

Gavin replied that they did something that the gang found very strange – they prayed. First, in their prayer, they said that they were there, not because they wanted to be there, but because God had put them there. The next two things that stuck in Gavin's mind was that the missionaries then prayed a collective prayer for their murderers – that God would have

MERCY on them, and that God would SAVE them. It was the words MERCY and SAVE that struck him. Then they killed those people with axes and left them lying scattered all over the hillside.

Gavin's gang continued their activities. A few weeks later two of his men were killed. A little later two were captured. That left thirteen of them – and most survived until the end of the war, eighteen months later.

Some time after the war ended, they were stationed in an army camp at Entumbane near Bulawayo in the south-west of the country. They were sitting together one Sunday reading a Sunday newspaper and their eyes caught the headline of an article which read 'Dear Comrade . . .' (All revolutionaries and combatants followed the custom of many atheistic nations in calling themselves 'comrade'). They read the article with interest, and it went on to say 'God loves you, Jesus died for you, Comrade.' It went on to tell the story of a Cuban revolutionary Marxist called Raphael, and as they read the story of his conversion to Christ, their reaction was to become enraged and infuriated. The advertisement (for that was what it was) went on to say that if the reader wanted to know more about this, they were to write to Margaret 'L' at Box . . ., Bulawayo.

They discussed this, and it was finally agreed that Gavin should write a long letter to Margaret expressing their great interest, and inviting her to come out to the camp to answer their questions. Having lured her to the camp, they intended taking her out of sight and killing her. Gavin wrote the letter and put it in the thigh pocket of his drill trousers and set off for the mailing point at the camp. On arriving there, he was surprised that he couldn't find the letter. (He didn't make any claim that a miracle had happened or anything like that.) So he scribbled another hurried note to Margaret and asked her to send further information! By return came a little Gospel of John, a booklet explaining how to give one's life to Christ and Margaret's own testimony of how she came to Christ.

Gavin read it all with interest. He obtained a Bible and began to study the Scriptures; at weekends he visited various churches and listened to the Word of God being preached.

Although it made sense, and all sounded very wonderful, he knew that he had sinned so deeply, and been such a terrible man (he had given his life to the devil) that there was no hope for him. Yet he kept on reading and thinking.

One evening a number of them were gathered in the barracks room when suddenly they had a vision. He was not hallucinating, nor was it something in his mind – but an objective reality out there 'because we all saw it'. They saw a vision of a Cross, and then it was as if the hand of God came out of this vision upon them in judgement. He cried out that God would have *mercy* on him and *save* him. (The words the missionaries had prayed!) God met with him and gave him an assurance of forgiveness and of salvation. Then there developed within him a burning desire to share this startling discovery with the former members of his platoon who had survived. He began to teach them, and minister to them. He prayed with them and, in turn, he led seven others (and this is perhaps the most incredible part of the whole story) to Christ. They all, all eight of them, decided to train for the ministry so that they could preach the Good News to others. The other seven had passports, and so hurriedly got out of the country (some to East, and some to West, Africa) and enrolled at bible colleges. But Gavin had no passport and had to stay in Zimbabwe. He too left the army and entered this Pentecostal bible college in Harare.

After hearing his story (and probably still in a state of numbed shock) Peter prayed for him. This man who had been the leader in the brutal massacre of God's people, people Peter had known and worked with, was now a brother in Christ!

After he got home, Peter told his wife that he just wanted a period of quiet so that he could accurately record the facts of a conversation he had just had. When he returned to the sitting room he found a visitor sitting there, a young man called 'C' who was a law student at the university. Peter told him he had just had the most incredible experience, and related all that he had heard. After he had finished, 'C' said to Peter, 'Describe the man.' Peter did. When he had finished, 'C' said, 'That's the man! Don't you remember? I was a student at Elim at the time of the massacre. The man you

describe is the one who called the whole school together and
gave us a political lecture that night.' Eight full-time missionaries had been massacred that night. Now exactly eight of
those who had done the deed had given their lives to Christ
and were in training for full-time ministry for the Lord!

Another pastor in Zimbabwe was able to clear up another
'rumour' for Peter. Pastor 'K' had been ministering at a
military nursing home at Nyanga (Troutbeck), where
seriously wounded men are rehabilitated, the home run by a
captain who had himself become a Christian. He invited
pastors to come in and minister to the men. As Pastor 'K' was
preaching, a paraplegic man in a wheelchair screamed and
cried out for mercy. After quietly closing the meeting, Pastor
'K' went over to minister to this man and listened to his story.
He was one of a group of guerillas who had massacred the
Elim missionaries. 'I led him to faith,' says Pastor 'K', and he
is now being helped further in his walk with Christ.

Jesus prayed that His murderers would be forgiven. Those
hardened and callous Roman soldiers, to whom the putting
to death of yet one more man would mean nothing, were
brought to faith by what they saw and heard. The centurion
summed it all up when he said, 'Truly, this was the Son of
God.' Stephen, the first martyr, also prayed for forgiveness
for his murderers as they stoned him to death. The worst of
them all was their leader Saul, 'breathing out murderous
threats against the Church.' Yet he, too, came to faith when
he saw a vision and became, probably, the greatest missionary of all time.

The Elim massacre was brutal. Those murderers had been
prayed for, that God would have *mercy* on them, and *save*
them. God not only answered the prayer of Jesus, but also the
prayer of Stephen, and the prayers of those missionaries out
on that cold hillside as they faced death. Out of the total
group of seventeen that perpetrated that deed, nine are
known to have repented of their deed and committed their
lives to Christ. Eight of those men set out to train for the
ministry. Gavin, we know for certain, completed his training
and is now part of an evangelistic team preaching the Good
News of Jesus Christ in Zambia.

As Peter said, 'There is no sin that is so deep that the love of God is not deeper. The only thing that God cannot forgive is the wilful rejection of Jesus Christ.'

Most surely, 'all things' do indeed 'work together for good to them that love God and are fitting into His purposes' (Rom. 8:28, Living Bible). God helped to put this kind of prayer on our lips through all the atrocities we heard about, perpetrated by either side. 'Father God, we don't understand why you permit such terrible things to happen, but we know that you bring good out of even the most terrible things engineered by the devil, and we praise you for the good that *will* come out of this. Amen.'

FIFTEEN

POWER OF GOD SEEN THROUGH ANGELS

There was a real flap on. Military intelligence had learnt that the largest ever guerilla force to enter Zimbabwe was about to cross into the country in our area – a densely forested and mountainous area. Many small 'details' or 'sticks' of men were out searching for signs of this group. A young Christian we knew, and his friend, formed a two-man stick, with radio, and were searching through their allotted section. They came over a hill and were well down the slope before realising that the thick undergrowth of the valley floor was 'crawling' with men. They had unexpectedly walked into the hide-out of nearly a thousand guerillas who had with them a small mountain of war material.

At the same moment, they too were spotted and a battle royal ensued. Our two young friends could only do one thing – dive into a small contour on the hillside, and start returning the fire. They started praying. Their radio was not picking up any friends. In moments, the three or four magazines they each had for their FNs were expended. They knew that only God could help them now. All of a sudden, they realised that all the shooting had stopped. Looking carefully out of their meagre hiding place, they were scarcely able to believe what met their eyes. The large group was moving swiftly back towards the border, leaving much of the heaviest material behind. In subsequent follow-up operations, one man was caught and interrogated. Amongst other things, they asked why the group had run off down the valley. The guerilla explained that when they saw the whole hillside 'alive' with soldiers in white uniforms, they knew that they were heavily outnumbered, and so made a run for it!

Escaping unscathed, our young Christian friend could scarcely believe that he was still alive. Then, a few days later, he fell off his horse during a period of R & R (a period of Rest and Refreshment granted to service men so that they could return home). As a result, he was hospitalised with a severe fracture of the leg, and was given a glorious opportunity to tell many people of God's wondrous doings in his life.

On another occasion when these 'soldiers in white' appeared, they brought protection to an elderly couple living in a lonely homestead. Feeling a little more nervous this particular evening, the couple knelt down to pray as usual before going to bed, and asked that God's angels would protect them from danger. In the early hours of the following morning a guerilla band attacked a neighbouring homestead a couple of miles away, and met with more than they bargained for. It was occupied by security force personnel! In the battle that followed, the security forces took, as prisoner, one of the men they wounded. In the de-briefing that followed, the guerilla explained that they had decided to attack the neighbouring farmstead, but when they got there, they found it surrounded and heavily guarded by soldiers in white, so they abandoned their first plan and moved against the homestead that – unbeknown to them – was actually guarded by the security forces!

A nurse who had been stationed at Nyanga also tells of an elderly man living on a farm nearby who was worried that it wasn't safe for him to remain on his land. However, he said that he would stay as he had a great belief in prayer. His servants told him that the guerillas hadn't attacked the house because they were afraid of the white figures guarding it!

Although angels are mentioned in the Bible – and my parents had taught me, as a small child, to believe that they stood guard round my bed while I slept – I had never really considered them as a reality in my own life. Can one really believe in them to actually protect one? I had not really consciously thought so. And yet angels in white – defending God's saints – have been reported in many wars in many continents all over the world. It was only as I came upon one incident after another in our 'own' war that I seriously began to question what I really did believe about angels. There was no doubt whatever, in Scripture, that we are told of a ceaseless battle going on in the spiritual world between God's angels, and the fallen angels who come under Satan's banner. Angels are often used as God's messengers – as they were to Zechariah, Mary, Joseph and many others. In the Bible, they are also seen as guardian angels, and guiding angels, and destroying angels, but I had never really thought of them, consciously, as playing an important part in *my* life – until various incidents in the war taught me otherwise.

Although no convoys operated on the Mutare/Harare road, for much of the war it was recommended that certain sections not be used after 4 p.m. Travelling as I regularly did to meetings in Harare, I didn't think it dangerous enough to take note of these suggested restrictions. It saved so much time if I got there and back all in the same day! However, because Jill finally asked me very specifically not to travel back in the evening, I then waited over and returned the next morning and often left Mutare in the early hours so as to get into Harare before breakfast. On one occasion, I must have left home soon after 3.30 a.m. As I approached the timber estates outside Macheke, I passed two large Swift trucks going in the opposite direction. Seconds later, a few minutes after 5 a.m., I entered the wooded section and, rounding a bend, saw the road covered in logs. No way would the little Toyota get over those. Braking hard, I was able to stop in time and – imagining a lorry ahead must have dropped them on the road – jumped out and threw enough logs off the road so that I could get through. Without further thought about the matter, I travelled on to Harare.

Early the following morning I set off for home. I stopped at the Macheke garage to fill up with fuel because the garage was owned by an old friend going through hard times with the loss of traffic. He greeted me outside and told me of a heavy attack they had sustained 'the night before last' in Macheke. The police station had been attacked with mortars and rockets, and at 5 a.m. the guerillas had fired rockets at two Swift lorries at a road block they had built just near the edge of the plantations! I must have missed them by minutes – or perhaps they didn't see me?

On another occasion, also very early and long before most people are around, I was travelling very fast with the wind against me. Probably for that reason the group never heard me coming until it was too late, but near a line of hills close to Nyazura I was surprised to see a large group of men off-loading bread and food from a very dilapidated van. Quite a number started to run back into the bush – but I didn't really think too much about it at the time. That night, a guerilla gang attacked Nyazura – from somewhere close by where they had obviously been hiding up – and tried to destroy the garage. Coincidence? Maybe!

The only time someone in one of our prayer groups tried to stop me travelling, was when I was due to take a funeral service at Chimanimani, about sixty miles south of Mutare through the mountains. There had been many ambushes on this road and a Catholic priest, much loved in the area, had been killed in one of these. At our prayer meeting that morning, I was told that someone believed my life was in great danger and that I shouldn't travel along that road. We tried once more to arrange for an escort to take us, but there was a shortage of men and vehicles. The funeral had to go on. So with further special prayers for protection, the undertaker and I set off with me riding 'shotgun' for him. He carried a revolver and I carried an Uzi. As we approached the bottom of one particular pass, I had a tremendous sense of the presence of evil – and prayed once more for our protection. Nothing happened, but on the way back, we found that the store at the bottom of that pass had been shot up and gutted by fire. Security force personnel were sure, considering the time lag, that those men must have already been in their ambush positions when we passed by the first time!

Twice in my life I have nearly written myself off in a car . . . but for the grace of God! On each occasion, I was travelling close to 100 miles an hour – I used to travel far too fast – and about to breast the brow of a hill, when some sixth sense (or guardian angel?) made me brake furiously just before reaching it. On the first occasion I stopped within inches of the first of a herd of cattle that had strayed on to the road. The second time I stopped within a few yards of a van that had hit an ox head-on, and vehicle and animal covered the

whole roadway. Whatever it was that warned me, I knew
that they were signs of God's special protection over me. But
angels . . .?

To my mind the matter was finally cleared up with the visit
of a well-known international Christian speaker and leader.
It had been arranged that after his visit to Harare he would
hire a car and drive himself down to carry out the next part of
his visit in Mutare. The scaremongers had obviously got to
him in Harare, for he telephoned and suggested that the visit
be postponed until some future occasion. I said that if he was
a little anxious about driving himself to Mutare, I would
come and fetch him myself. It was obviously an offer he
couldn't refuse! We therefore arranged for me to meet him at
a well-known hotel in Harare the next day – but I warned
him about the curfew on the road, and that we must leave
before 2 p.m. He was delayed for almost two hours, and it
was nearly 4 p.m. when we finally left town. At Macheke,
which we reached at 5.30 p.m., I showed him the large
signboard advising motorists not to travel on the next section
of the road after 4 p.m. I told him that I was quite happy to
continue through myself, but if he was anxious and concerned, we could stay with friends in Macheke until morning. 'I'm not worried at all,' he said. 'You keep right on.'

About fifteen minutes later, just as it was getting dark, we
passed through an area that we jokingly used to call 'ambush
alley' – a particularly appropriate name for a winding section
of the road through a great belt of rocky outcrops and hills.
Apparently our guest then began to repent before God for
unnecessarily putting our lives at risk, and asked God for
special protection. He believed he heard God say that I WAS
protected. On asking what that meant, our visitor was told to
look out of the car window and above it. He was shown the
most enormous angel spread out over the car with a flaming
sword stretched out ahead. This, he was told, was how I was
always protected! But the man never told us. He did relate
the whole story to a group in Harare, on his return, where we
had a number of friends! We believe that there was a very
special purpose behind those facts being revealed to us. You
will remember little Diana's deep concern over my travelling
out of town – particularly when she learnt I was not travell-

ing in convoy? Well, after this incident, everything was wonderfully resolved. I only had to remind Diana of the angel, and his flaming sword stretched out over my car, providing me with all the protection I needed, and she became all smiles again. All her pent-up fear for her Daddy was taken away. How merciful God is!

SIXTEEN

POWER OF GOD IN LITTLE THINGS

I had been a very heavy smoker for most of my life. When I arrived in Mutare I was smoking sixty cigarettes a day. Oh yes! I hated it, often, but there was apparently no way out of the hold that it had on me. I had smoked roughly fifty a day for over twenty years and was well and truly hooked. As a good Anglican, one of the things I had tried giving up 'for Lent' for a number of years was this dreadful habit. That Lenten penance was purgatory, but gave me a real sense of achievement and the wishful belief that, if I really wanted to, I could give it up anytime. That wasn't true. After a number of Lents without cigarettes, Jill and the children asked me *not* to do that any more, because living out their lives with me during those periods was unbearable! It was too much of a Lenten penance for them! And the last time I had given it up, I had put on 40lbs in six weeks, so I too was convinced that it was not a good idea to try that again.

In the old days, my smoking and the charismatic group in Mutare hadn't seemed to go together. For a start, none of them smoked and they never had any ashtrays, but in no way were they going to get me to stop. I saw no reason to stop smoking – except for actual prayer-times – while the Bible study was going on. I had a feeling that that irritated them, although they never said so, but I wasn't going to give them the satisfaction of stopping. Of course, if the truth be known, I had such a craving that I couldn't get through an evening without cigarettes!

Totally without my knowledge, half-a-dozen of them made a pact to pray for me to be weaned from my addiction. They agreed to pray for me daily until the habit was taken away. Each time they met they would ask each other if there were any signs that I had stopped. They prayed that God would take away every desire I had for the need for nicotine in my body, and that I would have such an aversion to cigarettes and smoke that I would never want to touch them again – *and* that I would feel positively nauseous in the presence of anyone smoking! Of course, I knew none of this at the time.

One night when we returned from one of 'their' groups, Jill and I were retiring to bed as usual. It must have been after midnight, but I still followed a new practice I had started of listening to a teaching tape before going to bed. The tape-recorder lay between us, and I was sitting up against the headboard, thoroughly enjoying one of the last cigarettes of the day. The particular tape was one of a series by David Pawson, delivered on successive nights, over a period of about a week. As this particular tape started, David referred to something that had happened as he was leaving the hall the previous evening.

'By the way' he said, 'as I was leaving here last night someone came up to me and asked if it was sinful to smoke.' (Don't you dare, I said out loud, taking a deep drag on my cigarette!) David continued on the tape, 'I can't tell you if it is sinful to smoke or not. (Thank goodness for that!) All you can do is ask yourself a question – "Is it of the flesh, or is it of the spirit?"' (Dear God!)

I knew the answer to that without a second's hesitation. Quite deliberately I lent over and stubbed out that cigarette. The unfinished packet lay by my bedside for over a fortnight – untouched! Although my very first waking act had always been the lighting of a cigarette as I rolled out of bed, I had no desire whatever for one the following morning. To this day I have never wanted to smoke another cigarette (and twelve years have passed). What is more, I cannot bear to sit in an enclosed space with anyone who smokes. It makes me positively ill. Nor can I 'stomach' going into a room permeated with stale smoke and uncleaned ashtrays.

I had started listening to David Pawson's tapes because I had learnt that he was an exceptionally good expositor of the

Bible, and I had already asked God to help me learn more about the Bible. I didn't feel threatened by David Pawson because I knew him to be non-charismatic! (Only later did he himself start speaking in tongues and amend his teachings on the subject of the Holy Spirit). Although I had problems with miracles – simply because many modern theologians did not believe in them – I knew that here was a real miracle. Only God could have taken away, so instantaneously, that craving (and my body's need for nicotine) in this way. But what really convinced me was this. Jill did not hear the initial start to that tape because she was still in the bathroom getting ready for bed. She knew nothing of my instant decision to stop smoking. Remember, I was not worth living with whenever I had previously been deprived of cigarettes!

Ten whole days later, after a dinner party in our house, Jill was handing out coffee to our guests. As she went past, a lady offered me a cigarette. I said, 'No thank you, very much.' Jill literally stopped dead in her tracks and said, 'I don't believe it! I've never heard you refuse a cigarette before! Are you sure you are all right?' When I told her I had stopped ten days earlier, she was totally disbelieving, yet all through those days she hadn't noticed anything! She hadn't noticed that all the ash trays around the house remained clean! She hadn't noticed that the smell of stale smoke, and the ghastly smell that comes from filled ash trays left overnight, had gone! She hadn't even noticed that I had not been smoking in all that time! None of the children had noticed I had stopped! I put on no extra weight as a result of God taking away my desire and need for smoke, and I had no 'withdrawal symptoms' as a result of coming off nicotine! Only God could have done all that.

Now I also have the perfect answer to anyone who asks the question, 'Is it sinful to smoke, drink, flirt, or whatever?' 'I can't tell you whether it is sinful. You simply have to ask yourself the question, "Is it of the flesh, or of the spirit?"' (Is this something God would approve of, or is it purely the satisfaction of a personal craving, an over-indulgence, or a lust within you that would in fact be displeasing to God?) No one can escape the consequences of that! I have had much cause to be grateful to those women who prayed so faithfully for me over that period of time, for David Pawson's timely question, and most of all, for the Holy Spirit's miraculous work within me that made it all possible.

To return to my spouse, Jill had undergone a really traumatic shock when her father suffered a heart attack and died. She was only twelve at the time and the eldest of three children. The family faced tremendous financial difficulties with the unexpected death of the breadwinner in the family. It was not helped by the fact that soon after her father's death – whether as a consequence of the traumatic shock or not, who knows – she began to experience epileptic fits. For a time it was thought that it was *petit mal* and that she would soon outgrow it, but it was later diagnosed as *grand mal*. The situation was not improved by the fact that many combinations of drugs used to try and control the situation had dreadful side-effects. Some caused a tremendous depression and others left her with a feeling of being perpetually 'drugged', or 'under the weather'. But as soon as she came to terms with her epileptic condition (and how difficult that is for anyone, let alone a petite, blonde extrovert bombshell wanting to enjoy life to the full!), and the right combination of medicines was found to keep the seizures at bay with the minimum side-effects and without depression, we began to see a positive improvement.

It was after we arrived in Mutare, after we had been 'born again' and we had begun to experience a number of miracles in our lives, that Jill's attitude really changed and we began to believe God could and would heal her completely. On numerous occasions special prayers for healing were said for her, including prayers and laying on of hands by those visiting the town and known to have a ministry in healing. Naturally, when there were signs that she was not totally healed (experiencing another seizure a month or two after believing she was healed), great disappointment would follow. We can never understand why, in some cases, conditions are not apparently healed after believing prayer. Ours is not to question why, but to trust that God knows best. Tremendous benefits have flowed from Jill's condition, not least my own understanding of the kind of traumas families undergo when an epileptic is discovered in the family. If on hand at the time, I can arrest the seizure and save Jill from all kinds of damage that so often happens during one of these attacks. And I was able to show other families what to do in similar circumstances.

We praise God for the tremendous amount of healing that *has* already taken place. Having experienced anything of up to one or more seizures a month, Jill has only had two in the last five years, and we thank God for the ministry to epileptics, and to their families, that it has brought us.

> St Paul tells us: But to keep me from being puffed up with pride because of the many wonderful things I saw, I was given a painful *physical ailment*, which acts as Satan's messenger to beat me and keep me from being proud. Three times I prayed to the Lord about this and asked Him to take it away. But His answer was: 'My grace is all you need, for my power is strongest when you are weak'. I am most happy, then, to be proud of my weaknesses, in order to feel the protection of Christ's power over me. I am content with weaknesses, insults, hardships, persecutions, and difficulties for Christ's sake. [The opposite of everything preachers of the Prosperity Gospel would have us expect?] For when I am weak, then I am strong. (2 Cor. 12:7–10).

Some contend that this remark, by Paul, had nothing to do with an *illness* not being healed, that we can and should expect healing for every illness and deformity. I also believe God created us to be perfect, and that He wants us to be whole. Yet sometimes *complete* healing *is* delayed, perhaps even beyond the grave, if that will be to His greater glory, because He *is* sovereign. A perfect example of this is seen in the story of Lazarus. He was sick unto death. His sisters, and probably Lazarus, had absolute faith in Jesus' power to heal. But He didn't heal him. He could have healed even from a distance, as He had on other occasions. But He didn't. Despite the faith to believe for healing, Lazarus was allowed to die and was buried. But much later, in an action that brought far greater glory to God and far more people to faith, Lazarus was raised from death and his sisters and friends received him back alive and well. Sometimes, for those called to wait, there is even greater glory to be experienced.

We have been privileged to experience God's healing power in all kinds of situations, but perhaps the one area that surprised us most – why it should have done I now find hard to understand – was in the simple everyday little things. A headache, a cold, a migraine, menstrual pains and the like. How easy to just accept that because they are so 'normal' and common, that God wouldn't want to be troubled with things like that! But He is! He made us perfect. He loves us, more than anyone else does. And just as a parent 'aches' for a little child with an earache or headache, or when burning up with a fever, so our Father in heaven is just as moved when He sees us screwed up with pain. But we need to ask. Scripture tells us that in all too many situations in life we do not receive, because we do not ask! And added to all this is the care and concern we have for one another. It is said that a problem shared is a problem halved. The same applies to our little illnesses as well. Just to have someone show loving concern for us brings a measure of healing in itself. And to know that they care enough to ask if they may pray for God's healing there and then shows how much they care. Many are even prepared to ask God to allow them to take the pain upon themselves – and so 'free' the person they love.

On many occasions I have seen Christians deeply disappointed when someone has heard of their 'illness' – promised to pray for them – and then walked off without doing anything about it there and then. Why? All too often because the person is shy or embarrassed at praying openly for the sick in public or out loud! What a tragedy to miss such a golden opportunity of really showing that you love and care for that person. And believe it or not, it is a fault most commonly found in priests and pastors dealing with members of their own flock! If you ever say 'I'll pray for you' – do it there and then!

Did you know that God can also 'heal' mechanical objects? Because Jill only had epileptic fits first thing in the morning, the medical profession never put pressure on her to stop driving. So what could a mere husband do? Nothing! In my previous education job I was away from home so much of the time that we had always had a second car. When we moved to Mutare, Jill kept it. It was a very special car to us. It was a real bargain for it had belonged to a little old lady who had bought it new and scarcely ever used it. When we bought it from her, it was six years old and had only done about 20,000 miles! Once in Mutare, I found myself continuing on our Diocesan Standing Committee in Harare and having to travel the round trip of 350 miles two, and sometimes three, times a month for that and other committees on which I served. The obvious choice was to use Jill's Toyota because we got an incredible sixty-five miles to the gallon out of it! With petrol rationing through the war getting more and more acute, it was a boon.

On one of these trips, with a car-load of people who were as newly excited about their faith as I was, the car began to falter and then go slower and slower as the engine ceased to 'fire'. Being miles from anywhere, I asked everyone to start praising God in song for what He was going to do to put this right! Just before it came to a complete stop it fired once more and on we went! We continued to sing God's praises! On the way back from Harare it happened on three separate occasions and, each time, started up again as we broke into praises to our God. We had decided by this time that there was probably a fuel blockage somewhere, and I resolved to get the car serviced and checked out when we got home. A service was long overdue. However, rushing off to work next morning in my own car, I never gave it another thought. Two or three days later I had to go to Harare again. It was only when we were well on the way that I remembered that I had failed to have it checked out. I 'confessed' this before God and asked Him to take care of us until we got home and I could get it done. I know God has a sense of humour! The car failed four or five times each way, and each time songs of praise to God got it working again! We got home safely.

The next morning I remembered my promise. As I sat in the car I thanked God again for bringing us home safely, started it up and drove round to the garage. The foreman was a good Christian friend of ours from one of the Pentecostal Churches. I told him what had happened, and the 'remedy' that had kept us going, and asked him to check it out and service it. About an hour later he asked me to come round. When I arrived he called one of the mechanics over and asked me to repeat my story. He said that the mechanic hadn't believed it from his lips. As I finished, the mechanic produced the 'points' from the distributor. He asked how I had got the car to the garage, because they had tried to move the car into the garage, but it wouldn't fire – and they had pushed it in. The points – absolutely unbelievably to the mechanic – had literally no points at all. Each end had the plastic type non-conductor sheet to which the points are fixed, but was otherwise clean as a whistle! I don't understand how it works, but the facts spoke for themselves! Jill also believes the car was capable of running on empty. We really could not afford to run this second car, hence the infrequency of servicing, and we could afford very little for petrol. Jill believes that for at least a week, at the end of each month before pay-day, she ran on empty. She never did any unnecessary journeys, but would ask God to just keep it going until the next pay cheque arrived. However, as soon as I gave her the money for petrol, if she tried to do one more trip before going to the garage for petrol, she *always* ran out and would be upset because she would have to telephone me to fetch a can of petrol and come to her rescue. The very fact that the car averaged sixty-five miles to the gallon – both on long journeys and in town – over a month – I believe speaks for itself. I never found another Toyota Corolla owner of that vintage who ever got more than fifty out of his vehicle. When we sold it, it was snapped up by a garage employee!

One of the great joys of living in Mutare was the never-ending stream of people who poured into our home seeking help. There were people who wanted help in family disputes and difficulties. People in a financial mess. People who just wanted a shoulder to cry on. Women unable to cope with running the family business because their husband had to spend so many spells away each year on police or army reserve duties. People wanting help because their fear for loved ones serving in the bush became intolerable, and every parting more and more traumatic. Even a woman suffering hideous nightmares every time her husband was on call-up. People trying to come to terms with grief. People needing healing. The break-up of so many marriages. The horrific growth of alcoholism as all too many lived on their nerves at 'the sharp end', where every turn in the road could produce an ambush or an unseen boosted landmine. (Were those pieces of cow dung lying on the tar road put there by guerillas to cover holes dug in the tar for landmines?) Men who came to us because, in a security mix-up between different units, one group of men had ambushed another, and killed and wounded their own people. Because of the kind of guerilla war that it was, men were shooting life-long friends in their own 'stick' during 'hairy' situations on dark nights. That is hard to live with – and even harder when you face the widow and children who are as close to you as your own family, and meet almost daily.

And there were still other apparent tragedies. There was the day a young woman was brought into our house in a terrible state. She had developed German measles at the most critical time of her pregnancy, and the doctors feared the chances of abnormality in the baby would be very high. Naturally she was beside herself with anguish. Would there be any point in praying for her, she wondered? We began to tell her of many miracles of healing that had taken place in answer to prayer, and asked if she had faith to believe in it for herself. She said she did. Both Jill and I, together with a Christian friend of ours who had brought her to us, began to pray for absolute protection of the embryo from any effects of the German measles. As we prayed, I was given an assurance in my spirit that she would be delivered of a perfectly normal child. However there was one thing that would be required of the couple. Each night, her husband was to pray with her and, with him laying his hand on her stomach, they were to praise and thank God for this perfect baby God had given them. I always found that kind of forward prognosis difficult to give! It was very much a laying of my own faith on the line! But the eventual birth of a very healthy, perfectly normal baby was a special bonus. With God, nothing is impossible.

Our third child to survive, Lynne, was a 'shock' to all concerned – especially to the parents! We had long since given away all our nursery furniture. But what a blessing she has been – a real *laat lammertjie* (late lamb!). She grew up in a home that was scarcely ever our own. She was used to watching people being ministered to. All too many poured out their hearts and tears. And Lynne knew what to do for the latter. Because we had no paper hankies in Zimbabwe, the next best thing was toilet paper, and away Lynne would fly to the toilet when she saw someone begin to cry. On one occasion, Jill had gone out and only Lynne and Leah – our domestic – were in the house. A young woman came to the front door. Lynne, only three at the time, invited her in because she looked so upset, and sat her down in the lounge. She then ran through to the toilet to get some toilet paper and returned and gave it to this lady, who was now really crying – imagining that Jill was being called!

Matter-of-factly, Lynne sat down in a chair next to her and asked if she was very sad. On being told that she was not feeling at all well, Lynne came across to her, put her hands on the young woman's lap, and said to her, 'Can we pray to Jesus to heal you?' Totally overcome, the woman said 'Yes!' So, without any further ado, Lynne shut her eyes and prayed, 'Jesus, please make this lady better. Amen.' Apparently the young woman just felt all the pain draining out of her. Lynne had total faith in Jesus' ability to heal! The woman left soon afterwards 'on cloud nine' and told us about it later! And that 'joy in Jesus' that has been such a mark in Lynne's life has continued. When we were in 'exile' in Harare after the attack on the cathedral, she expressed a desire to be able to pray 'in tongues'. A friend laid hands on her, at the age of five-and-a-half, and she was immediately given a most lovely prayer language in tongues. And it was during those dark days that she got a friend to write a letter to us, at her dictation, to tell Mummy and Daddy not to worry about anything, because everything was going to be all right! Out of the mouths of babes and sucklings . . .!

SEVENTEEN

POWER OF GOD IN SEEMINGLY IMPOSSIBLE REALMS

In order to speak of miracles that touched my mother's life, I need to go back in time. In 1963 my father had retired from the ministry as SGMO (Senior Government Medical Officer, or Superintendent) of Mutare General Hospital. He and my mother had been very distressed at the break up of the Federation of Rhodesia and Nyasaland and decided to emigrate to New Zealand, where he had been offered a post in North Island. It was quite a wrench after nearly twenty-eight years in Rhodesia. Before leaving, they had joined with Jill and I at our wedding in Gweru at the end of August. Unbeknown to us, they had been concerned about my mother's health for a little while and visited a specialist physician in Harare on their way down. My parents decided not to say anything about this, for fear that it would spoil our wedding! Three weeks into our honeymoon, we were called back to Harare because Granny Jess had had a severe fall and was dying in hospital. As we arrived at the hospital, my father called me aside and broke down as he told me the news about my mother. She had leukemia, her condition was critical, and they had cancelled their trip to New Zealand. My mother's great anxiety was for my youngest brother, twenty-two years younger than I was, and only six at the time of our marriage when this leukemia was discovered. Who would look after him, as Dad's life as a doctor would not make Robert's upbringing easy?

As we faced the situation and committed it all to prayer, I will always remember my mother's prayer: 'Lord, if it be possible, let me live long enough to take care of Robert, until he can take care of himself.' When she survived that first major assault of leukemia Gordon Brander, her physician, told us that it would return again in seven years. He himself had recently lost his first wife to leukemia. He had brought her through the first attack, but not the second. Treatment over that entire period kept Mum's condition stable – but right on time, seven years later, she began to go downhill again fast. Through all those anxious days there were many prayers for healing sent up. She was anointed with oil, and prayed for, in the cathedral in Harare. Miraculously, she came through yet again. Medically speaking I am told that very very few have ever survived that second attack. Over the next seven years her blood count was regularly checked, and careful adjustments were made to the medication to try and keep her stable.

She developed a new and wonderful gift. Painting. Our homes were soon filled with water colours and magnificent oils of the countryside and mountains she loved so much. Every day she lived had become an unexpected bonus for her. Daily, she rejoiced that Robert was growing up and now nearing the end of his high school education. By now my father had retired once more – this time from his private practice in Harare which my brother Alan had taken over – and they were living in their cottage in the Nyanga Mountains in the Eastern Highlands above Mutare. We had arrived in Mutare ourselves by this juncture. By 1976 her condition was very unstable and she was weakening all the time. Gordon Brander, that wonderful physician and friend, did everything he knew to try and restore her blood count to some semblance of normality, but without success. It must have been early in 1976 that my father brought her into Mutare for a regular weekly blood count. Even that forty-five mile journey was too much for her and she arrived exhausted. We spoke of the fact that we had, at that time, a special Healing service in our church one Sunday a month – and the next one was in two days' time. I saw the look of hope rekindled in her eyes and she said that they would come.

My father telephoned the blood count results through to Gordon Brander just before they left for home. Gordon said he very much regretted that he just had no further suggestions to make. It would now simply be a matter of weeks at the most. By the time they left for home, Mum changed her mind and said that she just couldn't face another journey down, and asked would we just pray for her by proxy instead, on Sunday. Even though Mum knew the end was now so very near, she refused to give up. On Sunday evening, they both surprised us all by arriving just before the service. My mother said she had felt certain God was telling her to be there, and so she had summoned up the strength to face another bone-shattering journey (to someone so frail) down from Bonda. As I anointed her with oil and we laid hands on her and prayed for healing, there was such peace in her face.

There was no dramatic change to see, but all through that next week she began to feel stronger and stronger. They came down on the Friday and there was a miraculous turn-around in her blood count. Gordon wrote to her afterwards and said that she must know that this time his medication had had nothing whatever to do with the change, and that God alone had intervened! How we praised God for His goodness to us. During the next three years she continued to run her home, painted many more oils, even visited England on holiday – the first time for thirty years, only her second visit since emigrating in 1936 – and generally astounded us all by her cheerfulness and zest for life. Because of the severe shortage of doctors during the war, Dad allowed himself to be pressed back into government service yet again – running the hospital at Nyanga and later helping at Gweru Hospital.

It was from Gweru that they came to visit us on their way to South Africa on holiday, and mother was taken ill in our house. They decided that after this holiday, Dad would finally retire and they would come and live in Mutare. The cottage and property at Nyanga were unsafe to live in. Several neighbours had been killed in attacks on their homes, many had experienced lucky escapes, and the general situation precipitated the withdrawal of all their friends to the security of the towns. (One farmer had an incredible escape. He and his wife were on their way to bed, when he slipped back into the lounge to read something. Being a man of habit, his wife expressed her surprise that he was not sitting in 'his' chair! Minutes later, a rocket smashed through the glass.

window and ploughed straight through the centre back of
'his' chair!)

Feeling a lot better the next day, Mum took Dad out and
helped him to choose, and buy, a small house not very far
from us. A day later Mum was in hospital. People who die
from leukemia often die slowly and painfully. Mum 'knew'
her time had come. A few days later, with her agreement, I
prayed with her for her release into the hands of Jesus.
Within a matter of hours of praying with her, we were called
to the hospital in the early hours, and she slipped peacefully
into the hands of someone she had always loved and served –
and who loved her. It was 19 July, 1979.

Her initial prayer to Jesus had been honoured. She had
lived long enough to see Robert complete his national service
and able to earn his living. God certainly answers our
prayers! And her length of survival as a leukemia patient set
something of a medical record – living as she did for sixteen
years after being given just weeks! Thank you Jesus!

Old 'Pop' Coventry was one of the grand old men of
Mutare, having been there from its earliest days. He was not
a churchgoer, and probably hadn't darkened the doors of a
church for many years, but his daughter Merry, and grand-
daughter Ning, were both Christians and deeply concerned
that he did not know the Lord Jesus. They were anxious that
he should be brought face to face with Jesus before he died so
that he could, as Jesus required of Nicodemus, be 'born
again' and be assured of a place in heaven. Try as we might,
we seemed to make no impression on him.

He was well into his nineties when he was rushed into
hospital in a deep coma. Ning asked me to come and pray for
him. Here I was back in one of those difficult situations that I
had so dreaded in my early ministry, but I had recently read
that people in a coma – and how often we hurt them by saying
things in their presence without recognising this fact – can
frequently actually hear, even though they might not be able
to respond in any way. So although Pop was seemingly
unable to hear or respond, I began to tell him about Jesus
and what He had done for Pop. Furthermore, I explained
that even now he could put his life right with God by
committing his life to Jesus. If he wanted to do that, I would

pray for repentance for him and pray the prayer of commitment for him as well. If he had understood all that I had said to him, and he really wanted to do this, I asked him to give us a sign by raising his right hand and arm. It was a devastating – and exhilarating – experience to see him painfully raise his arm and hand straight up, with such a look of gentleness in his face. That story, which I related at the funeral, moved many hearts and just underlined once again how good and merciful God is, and that nothing is impossible for our God. That experience has helped me in ministering much more confidently to others who are in a coma and seemingly unable to hear or respond.

It was Maureen Baisley who told me how much my prayers, readings from Scripture and regular words of encouragement had meant to her, when she was in a coma, after being blown up in a landmine on a convoy to South Africa. What particularly excited her was that I kept telling her she was virtually unmarked! Her sister Wendy, confined to a wheelchair and deteriorating fast from multiple sclerosis, was mercifully killed outright in the same explosion. The miracle was that Maureen and her parents survived. The car was so totally disintegrated by the boosted landmine that no one bothered to bring the bits back to town, yet Maureen was practically unmarked!

Tookie de Meyer, only recently arrived in our parish, arrived on our doorstep one afternoon in a very distressed state. It appeared that she had just had news from her mother in Johannesburg that her much younger, and dearly loved sister ('Gwinnie'), had epilepsy!

Probably the best therapy she could have had at that point was to discover straight away that Jill – who looked so well and healthy and perfectly normal – was also an epileptic! For many months we prayed with Tookie through the ups-and-downs of her sister's illness. We even had the joy of finally meeting Gwen when she came up to visit Tookie, and of praying with her. That period of time resulted in a close friendship between Tookie and ourselves. Naturally we were deeply concerned when Tookie herself became quite ill and was rushed into hospital with a suspected growth in her left side. She was operated on, but quickly sewn up again, because there seemed to be no way of tackling what turned out to be an enormous growth totally surrounding the kidneys – without radically damaging the kidneys themselves. Over the next few days, further tests revealed that one kidney had already been severely damaged and was no longer functioning – the second kidney was beginning to fail. Little hope was held out for Tookie by her physician, and the surgeon, the Medical Superintendent, Bill McGowan. Bill had become a great friend of ours and was a spirit-filled member of the Roman Catholic charismatic group in town.

All our prayer chains were alerted and everyone was asked to pray for a miracle. Tookie herself was fully briefed on all that had been discovered and her chances of survival. Her deepest anxiety was for her adopted son. She and her husband had adopted Ralph after both his own parents had died. Since that time, Ralph's stepfather had died and only Tookie was left. Ralph himself was still in Junior School. As she and I prayed together, acknowledging that Jesus was sovereign in this situation, her special prayer to Jesus was that He would let her live long enough to allow Ralph to be able to take care of himself. She found it such a special comfort to know that people all round the city were praying for her. Next morning, with her condition still critical, they decided they had to risk all on another operation to try and save the one kidney and see how much of the growth could be removed. An hour after leaving for surgery, she was back in her bed in the ward. Unbelievable as it may seem, they found the growth had completely disappeared and *both* kidneys appeared to be functioning. Further tests proved that both kidneys were in perfect condition! Bill McGowan was filled with wonder at what he had seen with his own eyes. And, of course, it gave Tookie a completely new outlook on life, just to know that God had loved her enough to allow her to experience a miracle of such proportions!

Quite a few years later, we were about to leave on holiday for South Africa. Tookie came to us and asked if we would allow her to follow us down in her own car, as she was a little nervous of the long stretches to the border. It was a particularly hot summer, and we heard that the area through the low-veld to the border was experiencing temperatures of between 120° and 130°F. To avoid that, we left home at midnight with the intention of arriving at the border before mid-morning. Unfortunately we had mechanical trouble and we were delayed at Masvingo for nearly seven hours. We left there at noon to drive the 200 miles to the border. About halfway, I was surprised not to see Tookie's car follow me over a slight rise. We went straight back and, being unable to find her car, began to search the bush. We discovered that she had presumably fallen asleep at the wheel, gone over the edge of a small bridge, and the car had then bounced back under the bridge and out of sight.

Both Tookie and her aunt had been killed instantly. It was a very sad time for all of us. Our own car was marooned because I was unable to get it going again. Jill and the children were given a lift back to Masvingo, with the bodies of Tookie and her aunt following in a police vehicle. I had to sit there in the 130° degree heat for four hours before a tow vehicle took me back to Masvingo – and there we had to stay. However Tookie's prayer, when in hospital and facing death, had been answered exactly. Ralph had just started work with an electrical firm in Mutare! Because this had been the answered prayer of both my mother and Tookie, I realised at that point that we need to be very careful about what we are praying for, because we get precisely what we ask for! Tookie, like my mother, was ready to meet with Jesus, and our one comfort at the time of her death was that she already had the assurance that God had bought a place for her in heaven. She had also told us on more than one occasion that she was now ready to go when Jesus called her. His ways are indeed past understanding! And there is scarcely a better promise in the Bible than 'Behold', says God, 'I have always loved you, so I continue to show you my constant love' (Jer. 31:3).

EIGHTEEN

POWER OF GOD IN GIVING (PERSONAL)

'Give to others, and God will give to you. Indeed, you will receive a full measure, a generous helping, poured into your hands – ALL that you can hold.' In fact, the same Scripture passage goes on to say, 'The measure *you* use for others *is the one that God will use for you*' (Luke 6:38).

Although I had realised that the Bible had much to say on the subject of giving, I felt that the Church had already done my duty for me by paying me less than a living wage! As a result I used to feel doubly good when I did actually give an average of £2 a month towards the Planned Giving or Sustentation Offerings in the church! And yes, our salaries were acknowledged to be scandalously low. When I was ordained in 1961 the stipend of a single priest was £43 a month. When I got married, our salary scales laid down that a wife was worth an extra £12 a month. Each child was 'worth' another £4 a month. For the next *twenty years* that salary scale remained virtually *unchanged*, despite the enormous increase in the cost of living over that period. From the very beginning we struggled to make ends meet. Admittedly we were provided with accommodation (pitiful indeed as it was in our first parish in Gwelo, and eventually heavily subsidised by my parents), and with light and water, and with some form of transport (or subsidies towards it). We only survived our first few years of marriage financially because Jill continued to work full-time in secular employment, but after Andrew's birth, when Jill was so ill, she was unable to look after or hold Andrew for several months – let alone try and go out to work.

Of course the 'free perks' did increase in value as the years went by, but the cash stipend that provided food, clothing and other essentials didn't. For quite a long period we were using nearly a quarter of our stipend on drugs for Jill, until free hospital medication was eventually provided – and most gratefully received!

It was an article on 'Christian Giving' by Bishop Alderson, which appeared soon after we arrived in Ruwa in 1966, that gave us pause for thought. Since Andrew's birth, Jill had not been working, and our one salary was so pitiful that we just couldn't make ends meet. Bishop Alderson's understanding of giving was this: because the state now performed many of the functions formerly dealt with by the Church, God's people were no longer expected to tithe since their taxes already provided many of the community service programmes previously provided by the Church. So his recommendation was that churchgoers should give – not one tenth (a tithe) – but a twentieth! Even that shook us rigid. We couldn't afford that, yet because we were desperate, we decided to try! Over the next few months our financial situation became even more critical.

The only thing that saved us was an unexpectedly large 'Easter Offering' – larger than we had ever received before. We failed to see at the time that it was a return on our 'planting' of seeds in faith. By carefully husbanding that 'windfall' we were able to augment our monthly stipend a little, as well as take a short holiday with our family, but the ugly spectre of school fees and school uniforms was also beginning to loom large on the horizon. How could we cope with that?

It was about this time that we attended David Neaum's church in Highlands for a Sunday Evensong. David's sermon shook us both rigid. He is a great believer in a number of fundamental teachings from the Bible. One of those is the necessity for God's people to tithe! However 'hard' his teachings on this subject, we found a ring of truth in them. No way could we find any biblical argument to contradict the fundamental truth of what he was saying. What was also important, David told his congregation, was that you should give your tenth to the work of God immediately you received

your salary, and it had to be a tenth of your GROSS salary –
and not of the net figure after tax and other deductions had
been made! (The tax didn't worry us – we'd never had to pay
any!) It had, he said, to be a stepping out in faith.

Jill and I had a very traumatic time after that sermon, for
both of us were totally convicted of the truth of David's
statement. How could we ever do it? we asked ourselves and
both knelt down and committed the question to God. At the
beginning of the next month, we would step up our giving
from £3 a month to £6.6.0, and we would pay it before we did
anything else! Surprisingly, to us, we survived, but only just.
Each annual Easter Offering (after being tithed) was carefully put aside to provide a little for a holiday and the remainder
went towards a monthly addition to our stipend – but it was
still a struggle, and we never had anything to spare. Remarkably, we managed to keep it up for the next seven years until
we went to Mutare.

There, through much sharing at Bible Study groups, we
reeled from one shock to another. We discovered that the
Jews were never absolved from tithing, however high taxes
were running. Jesus said, '. . . pay the Emperor what belongs
to the Emperor, and pay God what belongs to God' (Mark
12:17). Under the Romans, those taxes were considered
crippling. The tithes or freewill offerings of a good practising Jew would be not less than twenty per cent of his income. Furthermore, despite Roman taxes, Jesus not only
endorsed the law about tithing, but stressed it was simply a
minimum:

> How terrible for you, teachers of the Law and Pharisees!
> You hypocrites! You give to God a tenth even of the
> seasoning herbs, such as mint, dill and cumin, but you
> neglect to obey the really important teachings of the Law,
> such as justice, mercy and honesty. These [justice, mercy,
> honesty, etc.] you should practice, *without neglecting the
> others* [tithing of everything, even the leaves in the herb
> garden!] (Mat. 23:23 – such an easy reference to memo-
> rise!)

If taxation and other expenses provided no excuse for the Jew from tithing everything he had, then such considerations can provide no excuse for the Christian either . . .

The 'truth' that finally shattered us – revealed in a statement made by a friend in one of our Bible Study groups – was that we had never properly tithed at all! All that we had tithed was the smallest part of our overall income – the cash stipend – but we had never tithed our free 'perks'. We began to see that our accommodation, light, water and telephone bills paid for by the Church, and the provision of a car, were all part of our gross income, even though we never saw it in the form of cash! But how could we assess that? Light, water and the telephone were relatively easy. The Income Tax Department assessed what part of those were for personal use, and what part for Church business. They also put a value on the rent of the house which the open market could be expected to provide. We could argue that we would never rent that kind of house with our kind of income, but that was a red herring. We loved our house! And income tax also assessed the value of the private motoring we did in our official car. It can be imagined what all that added up to, and what a hole it would make in our cash stipend when we tithed it! Yet we were absolutely convinced that that was what we had to do if we were to be obedient to God:

I am the Lord, and I do not change. And so you, the descendents of Jacob, are not yet completely lost. You, like your ancestors before you, have turned away from my laws and have not kept them. Turn back to me, and I will turn to you. But you ask, 'What must we do to turn back to you?' I ask you, is it right for a person to cheat God? Of course not, *yet you are cheating me*. 'How?' you ask. In the matter of tithes and offerings. A curse is on all of you because the whole nation is cheating me. Bring the full amount of your tithes to the Temple, *so that* there will be plenty of food there. *Put me to the test and you will see that I will open the windows of heaven and pour out on you in abundance all kinds of good things* (Mal. 3:6–10).

And then God tells us something very important in this passage – something that explains why our money never stretches as far as we would like it to, and why we experience breakages, and heavy unexpected bills. God says to us: 'Then I will rebuke the devourer, so that it may not destroy . . .' (Mal. 3:11, NASV). What a tremendously descriptive word 'the devourer' is to describe the way things break, or wear out, or are destroyed by pests. It was an eye-opener to discover God could nullify those problems! It is startling what God can achieve in making everything stretch so much further. A remarkable example of this is found in the Bible when God's people had no other source of supply to turn to. Not only did He provide manna and quail to eat, and water to drink – most people know of those astounding facts, but are unaware of something else concerning that period – but: 'For forty years the Lord led you through the desert, *and your clothes and sandals never wore out*' (Deut. 29:5).

It is not without reason that Jesus speaks more of the essential need to get our money matters right with God than He does about any other single subject! And we do tend to worry more about money, or the lack of it, than about almost anything else. Yet, when we tried tithing everything we ever received, it worked miraculously. We have not often had luxuries, but we have never had to do without anything that was needed. Even more surprisingly, perhaps, we learnt that we did not even begin to give *anything* away until after we had tithed. Tithing was *not* giving. It was a return to God of what Scripture reminds us is rightfully His due. He gives us everything we have. None of it is ours. It is given to us in trust, and we show our thanks by returning one tenth of all that we receive as an acknowledgement that it is His anyway, and as a token 'thank-you' to Him for that gift. We only start to give to God or to any charity *after* we have paid our tithe to God. That is why Scripture talks of the necessity for tithes AND freewill offerings. Jill and I learnt in our own life that God expected a lot more of us, in the realm of giving, than just returning Him His tithe. And the more we have been lavish in giving in this way, the more He has given us to handle on His behalf! We even tithed and gave freewill offerings of what we might have considered ours – such as an income tax rebate. When God made it clear to Jill that she mustn't drive any more, we sold the car we no longer needed.

And before doing so, both of us felt convinced that we were to give away all the money we received to a particularly deserving cause that God laid on our hearts. When we sold the car, we were astounded at the price that we were offered. It was considerably more than we had paid for it some seven years earlier! There was even a momentary temptation to keep 'the profit' for our use! Nevertheless, we felt that it was some small 'compensation' for all the tithes we had never paid – and it was surprising (probably the wrong word to use?) how abundantly we were blessed as a family.

We shared with our children all that we did about tithing and freewill offerings. We shared the miracles of God's provision whenever it was seen. They 'saw' that it worked. When they decided to tithe their birthday money, they were delighted to find that much more arrived the next week. Should they tithe that as well, because if they didn't they could buy something they wanted? Again, they decided the tithe came first. The next week, the same happened again, and they tithed without a moment's hesitation. They nearly passed out when a week later they both received a totally unexpected gift for their Savings Bank of $150 each! They thankfully gave God His share of that as well.

Probably the most incredible experience of God's provision followed very soon after Jill and I made the decision to tithe everything – even our free 'perks'. It must have been about three months later when we saw an advertisement about the first enormous Renewal Conference that was to be held in Johannesburg. There were two very large stumbling blocks to our going. The first was that only those who received an invitation could attend, and we knew nothing of the organisers nearly 2,000 miles away in East London, South Africa. The second was the cost of the conference, the obligatory five-star hotel accommodation (the only kind of hotel blacks could stay in in South Africa, and part of the obligatory conditions laid down by the government for any multi-racial gathering), and the cost of travel to and from South Africa. We had nothing in any savings bank! Both Jill and I felt convinced that we were meant to be there, but that we were to trust God for everything. We committed those two problems to prayer, and decided that if we were to really trust

God, we must tell no one about the conference or our wish to be there.

The following morning, we received an invitation through the post from someone we had never heard of in East London! The letter had been well on the way when we prayed, but what about the money? That was far more difficult.

Two days later there was a knock on our front door. One of our parishioners stood there looking a little embarrassed. She said, 'I don't know how to say this, and perhaps you'll think me a bit of a crank. But in my prayer time I felt absolutely convinced that you are to attend a conference in Johannesburg that I was reading about last night, and I believe the Lord has told me to come and say to you that I am to provide all the money you will need!' When we shared what we had prayed about, she too was overcome! 'Please, you must let me know, then, as soon as you are able, how much you will need.' With that she left. Three weeks later we needed to send off our deposits. The lady in question arrived at our door again and reminded us that we still had not let her know the cost. 'But here is $70 to go on with.' Within a few cents, it was the rand conversion we required for our deposits.

I could not bring myself to tell our helper how much money we needed; it was something I just could not do. Jill said we had to! Driving round there to her house, Jill and I had such a furious argument over this issue that she insisted that I stop the car. She got out and walked off! We both finally arrived at the house in a fairly 'steamy' state – but I was adamant. I could not ASK for money. So the evening was spent talking about everything else but . . . A day later, we had to post off the rest of our conference and hotel fees. Our donor arrived on the doorstep at exactly the right moment again. 'John, you still haven't told me how much you need, but I think there is enough in this envelope to cover most things. If you need more, please, you have only to ask.' The amount was again accurate to within a few dollars. We posted it off. When another family heard that we were going, they thought we should make a holiday of it as well – with our children – and offered us their caravan. Another person then offered their truck to tow it. A few days before we were due to

leave, we realised that we would have to refuse the offer of
these vehicles. The petrol for the heavier combination would
cost us $60 we didn't have. We decided that we would
telephone the two people concerned the next morning, thank
them very much for their generous offer, and say we had
decided it would be less tiring to go in our small car and stay
with friends.

Somehow we got involved in several things the next
morning and overlooked the telephone calls. So during lunch
I finally went to make the calls and found a sealed white
envelope on the cradle of the telephone. It had exactly $60 in
it! Our God *can* provide everything He believes we need. How
we praised His name on this occasion . . . and many times
since.

Jesus went on to say, 'And so I tell you: make friends for
yourselves with worldly wealth, so that when it gives out, you
will be welcomed in the eternal home. Whoever is faithful in
small matters will be faithful in large ones. If, then, you have
not been faithful in handling worldly wealth, how can you be
trusted with true wealth?' (Luke 16:9–11). If we are faithful
in the use of money, THEN God will give us the true riches –
a new wisdom and understanding and power and authority
in Christ Jesus.

What God does through tithing is to draw us out of
ourselves. By obeying His laws about very natural things like
money, He not only shows us what miracles can happen with
things that we can see and understand, but through that He
leads us on to understand the part of His Kingdom we could
not see – the miracles of faith.

How often have we heard this argument? Do you believe
the Bible speaks about the need to tithe? Yes! Do you believe
the Bible to be the Word of God? Yes! Do you believe in
God's will for your life? Yes! Are you ready, then, to tithe?
No!

Why is that? Surely there is no other reason than that we
are not willing to start. Not willing, as God puts it in
Malachi, 'to put Him to the test'. Now if I am not willing to
start with the least that I have (money), then why is God
going to give me responsibility over more important riches?
So Jesus tells us to get that right and all the rest will follow.

It was James Duff in his book *Flashes of Truth* who said,

There are three kinds of givers – the flint, the sponge, and the honeycomb. To get anything out of a flint, you must hammer it, and then you only get chips and sparks. To get water out of a sponge you must squeeze it, and the more you squeeze it, the more you get. But the honeycomb just overflows with its own sweetness. Some people are stingy and hard as flint; they give nothing away if they can help it. Others are good natured; they yield to pressure, and the more they are pressed, the more they will give. But, thank God, there are still others who delight in giving without being asked, and it's the givers of this kind – cheerful givers – that the Lord loves.

Whether we are offering ourselves or our possessions to God, there's no question about the kind of attitude that is most pleasing to Him. He loves cheerful, 'honeycomb' givers who overflow for His glory and the good of others.

NINETEEN

POWER OF GOD IN GIVING
(CHURCH)

Members of the Church have failed to support God's work as laid down in His Word. It shouldn't surprise us, then, that the world does not respect us. It is said that an ardent communist will give everything he can to forward the spread of his 'faith' by giving every spare moment, by giving all he can of his income (considerably more than the tithers in the Christian Church), and by being willing to sacrifice all – even wife and family – so that his communist principles and efforts will help to convert the world. Most members of the Christian Church have no such dedication. Many have regarded it as little more than a social club. Very few indeed are concerned that not only most of the world, but also most of their relations and neighbours are going to hell when they die, because 'the Christian' hasn't thought it important enough to warn them of the wrath to come, or tell them how they can receive the gift of eternal life. The reason? Perhaps most of them have not been born again?

Nothing gives the Church a worse image than when it is seen to be continually pleading and whining for more money, or when large placards greet the visitor at some place of worship explaining that it costs £XXX per day to keep the place open, and that everyone entering this 'House of God' is expected to put 75p or £1 in the receptacle provided! And why should the world respect us when we ourselves, as Christians, don't respect God or His way? How true it is to realise that we show how much we care *by how much we give*! If our belief in Christianity has not yet touched our pockets, our wallets, our purses or our cheque books deeply and spon-

taneously – as honeycomb givers who do not have to be asked
– then does our religion really hold much value for us?

When I moved to Mutare, and had to accept the fact that I
was once more being called back into the full-time ministry, I
was determined that the things that had previously got me
down (and made me want to leave the ministry) would have
to change; if not, those things would break me. For instance,
I cannot imagine Jesus standing by and congratulating
church members who run church bazaars, fêtes, cake sales,
jumble sales and the like to subsidise insufficient giving
by their members (themselves included?)! Nor can I see
Jesus being delighted with a Church Council that requires
the vicar to sit outside his church all day for a 'Day of
Giving' to balance the budget, or to raise funds to repair
the steeple!

In Matthew 21, verses twelve and thirteen, we hear, 'Jesus
went into the Temple and drove out all those who were
buying and selling there. He overturned the tables of the
money-changers and the stools of those who sold pigeons,
and said to them, "It is written in the Scriptures that God
said, 'My Temple will be called a House of Prayer'".' Their
dishonest and unlawful practices (without any Scriptural
approval whatever) must be classed as theft, for in verse
thirteen Jesus said, 'You are making it a hideout for thieves'.
There was no need for the Temple to hold such sales, or to
make a quick 'buck' by insisting that people only put 'temple
money' in the plate. If the Jews gave as the Scriptures
required of them, not only would the tithes provide all that
was necessary to pay for the priestly ministry, but with the
freewill offerings added to them, the 'Church' could more
than meet the needs of the widows and orphans, the needy
strangers in their midst, and all the other social welfare
programmes they should be undertaking. But the leaders of
the Temple were greedy. They wanted more, and so creamed
off the profit of those who bought and sold in the Temple.
And it became more and more necessary to devise other
sources of income as more and more Jews, seeing the 'ungod-
ly' fund-raising efforts of the Church and the hypocrisy of
their leaders, saw no reason to continue paying their tithes
and freewill offerings as Scripture required.

I ask you, says the Lord, is it right for a person to cheat God? [That is just another way of referring to someone as a 'thief'.] Of course not, yet you are cheating me. 'How?' you ask. In the matter of tithes and offerings. A curse is on all of you because the whole nation [God's people] is cheating me. Bring the full amount of your tithes to the Temple . . . and PUT ME TO THE TEST and you will see that I will open the windows of Heaven and pour out on you IN ABUNDANCE all kinds of good things (Mal. 3:8–10).

Does that speak in support of a Church 'scrounging' for money? It certainly does not. But it does show us where to look for, and how to remedy, the problem. The 'thieves and robbers' in the Church need to recognise themselves for what they are. Uncomfortable? Yes, indeed! But then Jesus never did have any inhibitions about dealing with that particular sin in people's lives – publicly! He pricked the pompous bubbles of those who ostentatiously threw their £5, £10, £20 or £50 notes (or bundles thereof) into the Temple treasury by showing that their giving was utterly worthless in the sight of God. He said this about them because they only gave *what they had to spare anyway*! It really didn't cost them anything in terms of sacrifice! Only the poor widow, who put in everything she had (a total sacrifice), was praised by Jesus as doing something that was pleasing to God.

On 22 June, 1979, a very interesting article appeared in the *Church Times* in England on the subject of giving. 'Church people in the Diocese of York are being urged to give at least two pence of every pound of their NET income (after payment of taxes and national insurance) to their local church. This, it is claimed, will bring in enough money to meet needs at local and diocesan levels . . .' 'At present,' said Reverend Alan Bill, their stewardship advisor, 'people were giving a halfpenny in the pound. The 2p standard was a "minimum, duty level of giving". It could be achieved *without sacrifice*. But those who can are being encouraged to give up to 5p in the pound' (£1 for every £1,000 of income suggested by the Church Commissioners) '. . . General Synod last November asked dioceses to commend this to their parishes. But it was criticised at a recent York Stewardship Conference as an inflexible standard . . . it was also said to be *unrealistic*, asking for a five-fold increase in the giving level; and it would give the Church *more than it needed* . . .' (The emphasis is mine.)

I wrote to the *Church Times* on the subject of that article, and my letter was published as follows:

Sir, An article . . . entitled 'Flexible standards of Giving commended' has just been brought to our attention. It intrigued us for a number of reasons. 1) The recommendation was for an increase in giving to a level of *two pence in the pound of net income*. 2) 'It would give the Church far more money than it needed'. With regards to 1), we would be interested to know what Scriptural basis was found for this decision? And with 2), we must accept that we live a long way from England and have no right to make any judgements on what we read, but IS the Diocese of York really raising sufficient funds to a) pay all their clergy a living stipend/pension; b) maintain all their church/cathedral buildings in good repair; c) have sufficient funds to provide for new churches, etc. in developing areas; d) evangelise and reconvert England to Christianity; e) assist the work of evangelism/missionary outreach elsewhere in the Church? Perhaps in this last connection it is of interest to you and your readers to note that this Diocese of Mashonaland – with no endowments from the past – is self-supporting, despite the war that has been raging here for some time. This parish of Umtali (Mutare) now has a total membership of 560 families; many of these are nominal, but about half of these contribute something to the budget. We have a totally multiracial membership. We pay an assessment to the diocese of $678 per month. This pays a percentage of the diocesan overheads, together with the stipends of three priests working in missionary areas of our diocese. Umtali is a town on the eastern border of Zimbabwe/Rhodesia and one of the hardest hit by the war. In November last year, instead of visiting or canvassing our parishioners, we decided to send out a statement of what we believed God's Word was saying to us about giving. But, of course, 'promises' of an increase of thirty-one per cent are one thing; what results in actual practice is often a

sad reflection of 'things promised'. But God has blessed us
mightily (full statistics accompanied the letter). The results are staggering in any context, but in a war-torn land
the results can only be termed miraculous – because God
alone could have made it possible. We prayed that God's
Word would convict our hearts; we can testify that He has
been gracious . . .

To explain what happened, I need to go back to a period
about a year after I arrived in Mutare. With all the changes
that had been taking place in my own life, I found that I now
had to make my new position clear to members of our Church
Council – that I could no longer approve most forms of
fund-raising. As far as I was concerned there could be no
fêtes, bazaars, cake sales, jumble sales, or anything else of
that nature to augment Church funds. Yes, we had difficulty
in balancing our budget from the income that was coming in,
but instead of begging for money, we agreed to make every
effort to acquaint parishioners with the principles of giving
laid down in the Bible. From then on, we issued a special
brochure each year that set out to do three things: first, it
gave the income and expenditure for the past year on a large
diagrammatic chart; second, it set out what the Church Council thought would be required in terms of expenditure for the
new year (income was never guessed at!); and most important of all, the rest of the brochure concentrated on teaching
the principles of Scriptural giving. No appeals were made; it
was simply left to the Word of God in those teachings –
together with much prayer that went into the brochure's
preparation, and over it as it was sent out – to convict
people about their need to give to God's work, and at what
level. One Sunday a year, 'Budget-Offering' Sunday, the
preaching was also geared to teaching these principles of
giving.

There was something further that we did. Instead of
following normal past practice of waiting until the year end
to see 'if we had any to spare that we might give away' to
charities and other needy causes, we decided to be good
stewards of what was given to us each month, and to give
away a minimum of a tenth of our monthly income. It was

very clear to many of us that 'the measure we used in giving money away' as a Church, would be the measure God would use in giving to us! And that has proved true over and over again. The better stewards we proved to be in this connection, the more money God entrusted to us – because He knew that we would not use it selfishly for our own needs, but for the extension of the Kingdom and those in need. Rather than building up greater reserves 'for ourselves for rainy days', we had to trust Him to take care of tomorrow's needs.

Later on we were able to go a stage further. Giving away a tenth of what one receives each month does not involve any real measure of faith! So God showed us that when an urgent appeal came to us – and we believed God was expecting us to provide for that need – we did not wait until the end of the month to determine what the tenth would be and then give that! Instead we would, in faith, immediately send off what we believed was required of us, and trust God 'to make up' what we would now need to pay our own monthly accounts at the month's end. It was not unusual, when we took such a step of faith (oh, yes! it did cause anxiety to some who were used to looking at finances from worldly 'accountancy criteria') we would be wonderfully overwhelmed to find that our income would often increase, and totally unexpectedly, five or six times more than the average month. The net result was that we not only had enough to meet our own expenses, but even more money to give away again!

The reverse was also true! Whenever we found ourselves unable to meet our expenses, a quick check always revealed that we had 'overlooked' giving money away during the previous month or two. Even though to do so would threaten us with an even more serious cash shortfall, we knew first of all we had to give away whatever we had – to make up for what we had omitted to give away – and, hey presto! – in no time at all our income would rise again and our creditors would be paid!

These changes didn't happen overnight. Despite all the teaching that was undertaken in this field, many are still not convicted in this area of giving as Scripture requires. It was not uncommon, also, for someone to come and see me after receiving the annual Budget Offering Brochure and, pointing to an article on tithing, say to me 'John, why haven't you ever taught us this truth before?' When I was able to pull out brochures from the previous three or four years and show them that the same principles had been taught for a number of years, they would be amazed and have to admit that they had just never 'seen' this truth before! As with Jesus saying of people 'they will hear, but they will not understand', so is it also true that people will often 'read, and yet not have that spiritual truth convict them in their heart' until such time as the Holy Spirit opens their spiritual eyes! Sometimes it is just plain 'cussedness' on our part, because we do not want to face the consequences of what total obedience to God will entail in our lives!

They say that actions speak louder than words. Financial figures can have the same effect! (see opposite). It is staggering to see what God was able to do with a little group of people in one parish. There is still a very long way to go. My own estimate is that there were still only about thirty families tithing their income in 1985. However, given the tremendous number of people who emigrated during the war and after Independence, and the substantial numbers who transferred to other places in Zimbabwe, we lost an average of five or six 'tithers' a year from 1976 onwards. We also experienced a very painful fracture in the Church. Although I was seen to join 'the rebels' when I joined 'the charismatics' – for want of a better word – I felt that God called me, however difficult the circumstances for myself, to remain within the Anglican Church. What was more, I knew that I had to bend over backwards in trying to meet the needs and aspirations of the more 'traditional' members of the congregation, and to apply brakes on our enthusiasm and desire to change modes of worship too quickly. The net result was that I seemed to please no one! And so came a most painful parting with many whom I loved very dearly, who felt that the Church (as they saw it) was remaining static. And shedding tears they left for Churches which they believed were more open to 'the leading of the Spirit'. In terms of financial loss it was also staggering, because they formed the bulk of those who tithed at that time. However God provided many others to take their place, with scarcely more than a hiccup, and those who did leave have

SUMMARY OF PLANNED GIVING, GIVERS AND TOTALS

	Church Plate Offerings	\$1 to \$4 p.m.	\$5–\$9 p.m.	\$10–\$50 p.m.	\$ TOTAL	% of TOTAL
			Number of Planned Giving Families			
1975	\$2 300				2 300	17
		106			3 246	23
			43		3 132	22
				34	5 334	38
				1975 TOTAL	\$14 040	

				\$10–\$100 p.m.		
1978	3 060				3 060	17
		69			2 070	12
			32		2 220	13
				39	10 332	58
				1978 TOTAL	\$17 682	

1981	4 500				4 500	17.7
			55		3 198	12.6
				54	17 688	69.7
				1981 TOTAL	\$25 386	

				\$10–\$150 p.m.		
1983	4 500				4 500	13.9
			42		1 980	6.1
				60	25 800	80
				1983 TOTAL	\$32 280	

				\$10–\$2 000 p.m.		
1985	5 000				5 000	6.9
			58		4 000	5.5
				64	63 000	87.6
				1985 TOTAL	\$72 000	

SUMMARY OF TOTAL GIVING FROM PLANNED GIVING AND CHURCH PLATE OFFERINGS WITH COMPARATIVE NUMBER OF FAMILIES ON PARISH ROLL

YEAR	FAMILIES ON PARISH ROLL	\$ TOTAL GIVING	NOTES
1975	800	\$14 040	Large exodus during latter
1978	580	17 682 }	part of the war
1979	560	25 080 }	
1980	510	26 388	End of war: Independence of Zimbabwe
1981	480	25 386	
1983	450	32 262	
1985	430	72 000	

been wonderfully used in dynamic leadership in building up other parts of the Body of Christ. In addition, many of them later returned to the congregation.

About three years ago we estimated what income the parish would handle if everyone tithed his income – the minimum level laid down in Scripture. It worked out at a staggering figure of $750,000 per annum. And that only included those who were already 'planned givers'! Can we begin to imagine what a force Christianity would be to reckon with if that kind of resource were available to provide for many more full-time workers and equipment for the extension of God's Kingdom?

One of the reasons for the extraordinary increase in parish income came about, I believe, because of our commitment to give money away. We never, in fact, gave away as little as ten per cent of our income. In the first five years it averaged out at about thirty per cent, and the highest figure overall, in any one year since this scheme was put into operation, was forty-seven per cent of our total income. It is the principle that is important. The more lavish we were in providing funds for the needy and for the extension of the Kingdom elsewhere – often through denominations and organisations outside the Anglican Church – the more money God entrusted into our hands. Be 'stingy' or 'hard as flint', or selfish as a Church, and that Church will always be begging for funds. 'Give,' Jesus said, 'and it shall be given unto you.' And the principle God always adopts is that *we* have to take the first step and *give* in faith; and it is only as we show God the liberality of 'our measure' that He then responds even more liberally!

One of our members had run a business for many years. It always seemed to stay 'just in the red'. Every year-end statement, after taking into account things such as depreciation, consistently showed that the business was not making money. Once the owner gave her life to the Lord, this problem gave her some concern. After several of us discussed it, we decided the difficulty seemed to rest with the fact that the income of the business was not tithed to God – even though the business had been dedicated to Him. Tithing in this area was impossible because her husband was, if anything, a little antagonistic to Christianity at this time – and he held the purse strings. Even after he gave his life to the Lord, he would get a little hot under the collar if his wife suggested tithing the business income. His argument, understandably, was that the bank manager would never go along with such a principle while they still owed the bank a considerable overdraft! His argument seemed perfectly reasonable: 'You can't rob Peter' – the bank manager – 'to pay Paul' – God!

However, as the husband's own commitment deepened, he finally agreed that they should tithe the income of the shop to God, as provided for in Scripture. The result was, in their eyes, unbelievable. Nothing happened overnight, but in a matter of a few months they were out of overdraft, and the business went from strength to strength. God's ways ARE beyond our understanding; but the principles are His – and they work! The same happened to a farmer and his wife. Soon after purchasing the farm, they ran into deep financial trouble. They made a deep commitment of their lives to God and heard about tithing at one of our Bible Study groups. They started to tithe everything that came off their farm. Very soon, although the farm fell in the rain-shadow of the mountains and often experienced difficulties with irrigation, the farm was being described as the 'green oasis' in that belt of country. On one occasion they were so short of cash that they could not provide insecticide to deal with a great invasion of pests, which threatened to wipe out the whole crop. The couple turned the problem over to God in prayer. Next day their neighbours hired aircraft to come in and spray their own crops. What happened? All the birds from the neighbouring farms were driven on to the farm of the Christian couple, and they rid the farm of the pests without an ounce of insecticide being purchased! On another occasion the drought was so severe that the areas which farmers could irrigate was severely limited. This young couple planted two lots of crops which they needed desperately to continue servicing their loans. The one lot was irrigated, the other was not. The one that was not irrigated they called the Lord's crop. All through the season the rain was very meagre indeed, and they wondered if the irrigation would even hold out for the land they were allowed to irrigate. As it turned out, the Lord's crop – which had no irrigation whatever – turned out to be the best crop of sorghum they had ever had on the farm.

The same principles worked miraculously for us in the parish. We never had to hold any 'sales', or use any 'gimmicks' to raise money – even for the major expense of maintaining a large number of properties, all of which were regularly attended to on a planned five-year cycle. In 1985 we already had two full-time priests working in the parish. At short notice, and without having budgeted for it, we were able to offer an additional full-time post to one of our lay men. His salary, the cost of an extra house and vehicle to be provided for, was beyond what was available monthly at the time we engaged him. However, we believed we were doing what God wanted us to do, so no appeals were made to the parish to step up their giving. Not only were we able to meet all the additional costs, but our level of 'giving money away' was still maintained at over thirty per cent of the total for that year. God indeed takes care of the 'things of tomorrow'!

TWENTY

POWER OF GOD IN EQUIPPING THE SAINTS

In 1977 ours was the first Anglican parish in Southern Africa to experience a Lay Witness Mission. Lay Witness Missions (LWMs) are run with the support and guidance of 'Africa Enterprise', an organisation set up under the leadership of Michael Cassidy and Bishop Festo Kivengere. Their primary concern, as an organisation, is to carry the Good News throughout Africa. An LWM takes place in a parish or congregation after six months of intensive preparation within that congregation. Then a group of lay witnesses from many different Churches and Church backgrounds (after suitable training by Africa Enterprise LWM staff) arrive for the weekend. One important principle governing such witnesses is that they must meet their own travel expenses when taking part in such weekends. It is a mark of their commitment to share the Good News with others. One such group recently went all the way from Zimbabwe to Australia to conduct two LWMs, and another group travelled from South Africa to Canada!

After the arrival of the lay witnesses, large meetings of the whole congregation are held on both Friday and Saturday evenings around a communal fellowship meal, with a number of witnesses sharing their testimonies of what God has done to change their lives. Then the whole crowd is divided into small groups under the leadership of the visiting witnesses, and people are brought to a deeper understanding of what the Gospel is all about, and of their need to respond to it. 'Coffee Groups' are held in people's homes on the Saturday morning, and these are followed by 'women's only' and 'men's only' lunches.

The mission ends with a time of worship on the Sunday morning, and a personal testimony and challenge given at that time by the leader of the Lay Witness Mission, himself a lay person. He makes a call for every member of the congregation 'to give as much of himself as he can, to as much of God as he understands at that point in time'. Our LWM was an outstanding success, with many lives radically changed for God. Because of its success, and the large influx of new faces in our congregation, a second LWM was held in the parish just over two years later.

That first Lay Witness Mission was ably organised by Chris Sewell, who had been appointed as a full-time lay minister in our congregation when my assistant priest, Leslie Crampton, was appointed Rector of Masvingo. We worked well together. Chris had been a member of the CID in the police. He was such a 'hard nut' in the eyes of a former colleague of his – a Pentecostal pastor – that Chris was placed at the bottom of that man's list of possible 'converts' because he considered it unlikely that Chris could *ever* change. With God, fortunately, nothing is impossible! Chris gave his life to the Lord in fairly dramatic style, was baptised in the Spirit, and became a leading light amongst that renewed group that I found at St John's on my arrival in 1975. It was soon after my own life-changing experience that Chris felt the call of God to resign from the police and work full-time for the Lord.

Such a ministry, that of a layman, has its drawbacks. In the Anglican Church any 'Lay' ministry is limited in what it can undertake. The lay minister can never carry out functions that are 'reserved' for the ordained priest; the Church will not permit it. So, although the task of the Church is to train *all* its members for ministry (Eph. 4:12), the dichotomy remains. A layman, however well trained, however richly endowed in gifts of the Spirit and gifts of ministry, must always remain a 'lay' person unless he is willing to be ordained a priest. Only then can he 'break bread' at the Lord's Table for the family of God. But the roles can never remain interchangeable. Once the die is cast and he is ordained, he finds himself automatically separated from what tends to be regarded as a second-class ministry within a layman's group.

The Church is all the poorer for this attitude. Very early on in the Church's life – certainly by the second or third century – this led to the establishment of a 'separatist' professional ministry. Soon afterwards, it was expected to do almost all the work of ministry in the Church, with the lay person bowing out of ministry almost altogether, and surrendering his God-given talents and responsibilities. This group eventually became content to be little more than pew-warmers on a Sunday morning. Satan had indeed won a dramatic victory! Instead of having to work against a whole congregation mobilised for ministry and evangelistic outreach, he was now able to concentrate his efforts against only one man in each congregation.

As Anglicans, there were problems over believers' baptism. Chris and his wife Helga felt totally convinced that God was calling them to take that step. This made it impossible for Chris to continue serving in ministry while the bishop's licence remained an essential requirement for him to be able to do so. So Chris had to leave, and we were really thrilled when he was appointed as the leader of Africa Enterprise in Harare with a much wider, fuller and, in many ways, more satisfying ministry.

One of the most important effects of the LWM was the desire born in many hearts to share their faith with others as the visiting lay witnesses had done. As a result, training weekends were started for those members of our congregation who wanted to become witnesses with the LWM team. The majority of these people are still actively witnessing whenever able to do so. They witness in Churches of all denominations when called upon to do so by the LWM organisation. They have shared their faith with members of many different denominations, and with unbelievers, in cities, towns and villages across the length and breadth of Zimbabwe, and even further afield – all at their own expense. They have seen many lives changed, and that has done much to encourage them.

One Scriptural principle that I took to heart very early on in my 'renewed' ministry in Mutare was that my two primary roles in the ministry were to i) bring people to a knowledge of the saving power of the Gospel and, ii) to equip the *whole* Body of Christ for ministry.

> And He [Jesus] gave some as apostles, and some as prophets, and some as evangelists, and some as pastors and teachers, for the *equipping* of the saints *for the work of service*, to the *building up* of the body of Christ; until we *all* attain to the unity of the faith, and of the knowledge of the Son of God, to a *mature* man, to the *measure* of the stature which belongs to the fulness of Christ . . .

Then, St Paul tells us, 'the *whole* body, being fitted and held together by that which *every* joint supplies, according to the proper working of *each individual part*, causes the *growth* of the body for the building up of itself in love' (Eph. 4:11–13, 16, NASB).

There was one complaint that we continually seemed to be bringing before the Lord. Why did He take away all those we trained almost as fast as we trained them? With the large exodus from the country during the war and immediately after Independence – coupled with Zimbabwe's ever present problem of a large part of the population being liable to transfer around the country on promotion – we seemed to spend our time continually training new leaders to train others. Some did not leave us and began to feel the pressure of continually training new leaders. People like Jean and Giles Wakeling, Bill and Liz Reynolds (Bill being the second full-time lay minister in the congregation), Gwynne Palframan, Barbara Shepherd, my wife Jill – and so many others. God soon showed us there was a purpose. We were to think of ourselves as a 'Maternity Unit'! Our task was to continue training people as witnesses, evangelists, Bible study leaders, and equippers so that they might be sent out all over Zimbabwe and further afield to serve the Lord in His Church – whether in the Anglican or the wider Church.

The excitement of having people trained as witnesses led us on a step further, to something the Anglican Church has never been particularly noted for – training lay evangelists fully equipped to i) share the Gospel with unbelievers; ii) bring those people to commit their lives to Christ; and iii) train those new converts into becoming not only soul winners, but trainers of yet more soul winners for Christ. While continuing to build up the Body of Christ God had already given us (using a number of courses devised by ourselves and others), much prayer and thought was given to how we might train evangelists who would carry out these functions. In this connection, Gwynne Palframan returned from a holiday in South Africa bearing a book she had found entitled *Evangelism Explosion*.

Although excited by it, we felt it was 'too American'. I adapted our own training course to the principles laid down in the book. It was, my trainees told me, the best course we ever did. I believe it was the excitement of presenting the Gospel to someone – with results – that did us a power of good! We had actually achieved a breakthrough in something almost all of us find difficult to do – sharing our faith *effectively* with others.

Later on I was able to attend an Evangelism Explosion Clinic and have myself 'certified' (American terminology for certificated!) as an EE Trainer. Before long I was helping with EE clinics (a five-day concentrated course equipping pastors and their lay leaders to start seventeen-week courses in their own congregations) in Soweto, in South Africa, and in Bulawayo. Soon our own parish was approved as a second clinic base for Zimbabwe and I was, in due course, accredited as a clinic teacher. To this base in Mutare I was able to bring in pastors and priests from Mozambique, Malawi, Zambia and Zaire – as well as from all over Zimbabwe – to be trained and equipped for evangelism. I also had the privilege of visiting Zambia on a number of occasions to encourage the work of evangelism there.

The most exciting field, to me personally, was our own city. After we had trained about twenty people in our own congregation, word began to get about the city that the Anglicans were doing very 'un-Anglican things'. Regular teams were visiting unbelievers in their homes, sharing the Gospel, and bringing people to Christ! As a result of this, two members of a Pentecostal church came and asked if I would train them! I agreed to do so with the approval of their pastor. Before very long we had pastors and lay people from almost every denomination in town training under our leaders. The richness and joy of our fellowship was one of the most memorable aspects of it all. When one shares so much of oneself with a member of another Church for seventeen weeks of concentrated study, checking of homework, and visiting together to share the truths of the Gospel with unbelievers – tremendous bonds of fellowship develop. For quite a long time we had a truly unique experiment in progress. Teams of three (the usual EE practice so that trainees get 'broken-in' slowly by more experienced people) would be drawn up on a multidenominational basis. When one of these teams brought a person to the point of making a commitment for Christ, you might well imagine that the team would have a problem in deciding which Church the new convert would now join. In fact we left it to God to lead that person to a Church of his own choosing, and the team would simply try and 'nourish' that person's development until members of the 'new' Church took over the responsibility.

Probably one of the many well-worn excuses used by so many when challenged with the Gospel message is, 'How can I know which Church is the right one? You are all so divided!' This excuse quickly fell away when the person visited discovered that the group was representative of different Churches and, even more important, able to show that all the Churches taking part in this exercise were in agreement on all the most important aspects affecting the proclamation of the Gospel of Salvation!

I have to be honest and admit that I had never been trained to actually lead anyone to Christ. Certainly not at theological college, nor with anyone with whom I had worked in the ministry. I had taught lots 'about' the Gospel, 'about' Jesus. But to actually sit down with an unbeliever, or with a member of the Church who was unclear about his salvation and be able, in a concise form, to present the Gospel of Salvation in such a way that would convince the hearer of his need to repent, and point the way clearly to what he had to do to get his life permanently right with God – that was something I had not known how to do.

The greatest experience in my life came when, after nearly sixteen years in the full-time ministry, I was able to sit down with an unbeliever I didn't know from Adam and, in a couple of hours, share the Gospel in such a way that he committed his life to Jesus Christ! Obviously the work was done by the Holy Spirit, but I had been given such clarity concerning the Good News Jesus had to offer the listener, that he was entirely convinced. The indescribable joy of that moment brought home to me in a new way that Christ never intended us to 'hug our faith to ourselves'! 'Go in to all the world,' Jesus said, and share your faith. St Paul says much the same when he tells us that we need to be able to give a reason for 'the hope that is in us'. It is nothing very difficult, he says. You don't require university or theological degrees before you can be set loose on the world. Far from it. All you have to be able to do is to tell of the great things that God has done in *your* life. And the most important is how Jesus came to give you new life with Him for ever – starting right here in this life, living a transformed life by the power of the Holy Spirit! (Rom. 15:18,19).

Of course we had some difficult moments over sharing the Gospel with strangers. There were times when we were abused and ridiculed, and had doors slammed in our faces, but they were rare indeed. One of the remarkable features about Africa today is that the 'fields are white unto harvest', and Jesus is sending forth labourers into the harvest He spoke about, in order to reap it. In our own experience in Mutare over a seven year period, and in all our clinics in Zimbabwe (and the ones I attended in South Africa), over fifty per cent of the people who heard the Gospel presented to them made a commitment to the Lord Jesus. That is a staggering, but very exciting, fact!

There was one thing that we learnt very clearly. The Gospel has the power to change lives in every strata of society. God is no respecter of a person's wealth, educational ability, or status – or lack of any one or more of them. The 'same' Gospel has the power to convert both the academically brilliant and the humblest person from the slums.

My wife tends to have a persistent streak in her! One night as our groups were getting ready to go out on our evangelism

visiting programme – and all the visits had already been
decided upon – Jill suddenly said, 'I believe God wants us to
visit Mr X.' A shocked silence followed. One could almost
'feel' the response of the group leaders – 'Well, I'm not
offering for that impossible assignment. Anyway, I already
have a visit lined up!' I was foremost amongst them, for the
man was a well-known leader in the community, a great
intellectual, and known to be somewhat antagonistic towards the Christian community. So I told Jill, that as no one
offered, God obviously did not want us to go there that night!
Jill does not give up easily. The following week the same
thing happened. Again no one volunteered, and so her
suggestion was put aside.

Believe it or not, knowing that she was probably antago-
nising me by doing it, but convinced in her own mind that
God had laid that person's name on her heart, Jill then
brought it up for the third week running. Following my
natural human instinct, I was angry with her because it
seemed to show me up as a coward who was not willing to
tackle this tough case. But, of course, she was absolutely
right! In my anger, and to silence her persistence and any
suggestion that I wasn't brave enough to tackle this assignment, I said – with a fair degree of bad grace – 'All right! I'll
go!'

I faced some bad moments before reaching that house, and
after entering it. And we did have a very hard time of it. For
two hours and more every intellectual argument that he
could think of, all his scoffing at the hypocritical types that
went to church, were thrown at us. Eventually, I was able to
make a presentation of the Gospel to him, and to share what
Christ had to offer him as an individual, someone Jesus died
for and still loved. Obviously we had an enormous back-up of
prayer going on through all our support groups at the time.
They knew where we were, and no one was under any
illusions as to the difficulties they knew we would be experiencing. But God is fantastic. That man's heart was
changed. 'I will remove your heart of stone, and give you a
heart of flesh' (Ezek. 11:19).

He was, deep down within himself, looking for something
that would really satisfy him. He gave his life to Christ that

night as we prayed together, kneeling on the carpet in his lounge. And what peace and joy filled that room as we talked and shared together afterwards over a cup of tea. How we praised God as a Christian community later that night! And how grateful I was for Jill's persistence!

On another occasion one of our teams arrived at the home of one of our black doctors. They got a very warm welcome, but the hearts of the evangelists began to 'freeze' as they heard this man relate his story. He had spent nearly fifteen years in Russia training to be, and practising as, a doctor. He had been thoroughly indoctrinated by the communists. What a challenge! Despite the apparent obstacles, and with their 'heart in their mouth' at times, they went ahead and shared with him the things that had radically changed their own lives for the better, and which had given them something to live for. They shared what the Gospel of Salvation had to offer. The man admitted that communism and all the other ideologies he had tried had never satisfied him. Hearing the Gospel presented that night, so clearly outlining what God had prepared for those that loved Him, convinced him that he had at last found what he was looking for. He surrendered his life to Christ. Stranger than fiction perhaps, but a week later he was rushed into hospital, very ill. By the time they discovered the very unusual complaint he was suffering from, it was too late to save his life. Yet he died with the certain knowledge – something he had not had ten days before – that he would be with Jesus in heaven for ever! We seldom realise how short someone's time might be, so no wonder St Paul reminds us, however much we might 'ruffle someone's feathers' in doing so, to preach the Gospel 'in season, and out of season' (2 Tim. 4:2).

Another visit that really challenged one of our teams took place one night as they were undertaking door-to-door evangelism in a block of flats. One door was opened by a young person who immediately invited the team in. As soon as they got inside they realised that here was someone who was very much a supporter of the new Independent Zimbabwe. The walls were covered with the new Zimbabwe flag, together with great big posters of Robert Mugabe our prime minister. They congratulated him on his enthusiasm for our lovely country. It turned out that this man had spent much time outside the country during the war, and had returned as a political commissar. As such, he had responsibility for indoctrinating the local proletariat (us, the people) with communist ideology, and the Marxist-Leninist doctrines adopted by our new government. Nothing daunted, the Gospel was presented. Perhaps not so surprisingly, the person concerned revealed that he had become a little disenchanted with the 'earthly paradise' that had been promised and which showed little sign of materialising. In contrast, the Gospel, and what it had to offer in both this life and the next, really made an impression on him, and he decided to give his life for Jesus.

Over the seven years that the evangelism programme was in operation, (until we left) a great many of our people – together with pastors and leaders from many other Churches both within and outside Mutare – had a tremendous sense of achievement in being equipped to share God's Good News with others effectively. There can be no greater joy, in obedience to Jesus' direct command, than in seeing someone brought into the Kingdom.

TWENTY-ONE

POWER OF GOD IN SPREADING THE GOOD NEWS

I have been told on good authority that a great preacher, with a recognised prophetic ministry, prophesied in Rhodesia just after the Second World War that 'many years hence' a revival would sweep through Rhodesia and that it would begin in the little border town of Mutare. In 1972 a small group of Christians were meeting together in that same town. Barbara Shepherd, a long-time member of our congregation, told me that it was at about the time that people in the congregation began to be 'baptised in the Spirit', and 'speak with tongues'. The small group had little experience of the prophetic ministry – particularly the kind when someone stands up and says, 'Thus saith the Lord ...' A stranger walked into their group that night and spent the evening with them. In the middle of the meeting he was given a prophecy – and he shared it with them: 'In ten years a light will go out from this city that will transform this nation and the nations round about.' Ten years ahead seemed far, far away, but Barbara, being that kind of person, recorded the prophecy. For a number of years it was virtually forgotten.

In 1982, all the Churches in Mutare joined together in a mammoth city-wide Christian campaign called 'Mutare for Jesus', or *'Mutare kuna Jesu'* in the Shona language. After months and months of preparation, an enormous Africa Enterprise team, nearly forty strong, flew into Mutare under the leadership of Michael Cassidy. They represented eight nations including Kenya, Uganda, Tanzania, England and the USA. For three weeks every part of our community in

Mutare and the outlying country districts was contacted. Many people gave their lives to Christ as teams visited schools, businesses, industry, farms, the police force, and churches. A quite incredible outreach was also started amongst the various army encampments in the area. This was a very sensitive area indeed, with the government doing its utmost to try and mould together three former armies that had, until a short while before, been in confrontation with one another – the ZANLA, ZIPRA and Rhodesian armies. Many thousands of Bibles were distributed in these camps (and elsewhere) at public meetings where, to obtain one, the men had to stand up and ask for a Bible in front of all their peers! Quite a number committed their lives to Christ. During the main week of the campaign, when major rallies took place nightly in three separate sections of the city, six thousand people committed their lives to Christ. The majority of these were first time commitments! The city and province were dramatically affected by that campaign. It was so well publicised that almost no one in the province was unaware of what was taking place. At one night's meeting in Sakubva, almost the entire crowd of two thousand responded to a 'call'. The speaker knew they could never cope with that number. Amongst other things, he noticed that most of those sent in by the Churches to act as counsellors – obviously only nominal Christians themselves – also came forward to give their lives to Christ! The only thing he could do was to spell out exactly what a really radical commitment to Christ would entail – including renouncing trust in charms, visits to witchdoctors, and the like. The number that finally responded to that radical challenge was still large, but manageable!

Great care had been taken by our Shona pastors to decide exactly what Shona word should be used in our mission title. '*Mutare KUNA Jesu*' was finally chosen as being closest in meaning to 'Mutare FOR Jesus'. There are many different dialects among the Shona groups, so it is all too easy to use a word that will mean something entirely different to one of the Shona tribes. Despite all the care that was taken, this happened over our title! A group in a remote area about a hundred miles south of Mutare really caused the local pastors a hard time. To them the title '*Mutare KUNA Jesu*' meant that Jesus was going to be physically present in Mutare, and hundreds were pestering Church leaders for appointments, personal appointments, with Jesus in Mutare! They might be excused for thinking such thoughts. Mutare was in such festive mood for the occasion that the City Fathers agreed to our request – and at our expense – to line the main street right through the centre of the city with coloured lights and bunting. Great banners across the streets, both in the centre of town and on the approach roads from outside, together with thousands of red and white posters, gave the city a festive air that no one could fail to notice. However, a cabinet minister's visit to the city days before the start of the campaign proper put paid to the coloured lights and the bunting. He ordered the City Fathers to take them down as they were only to be used on 'national' occasions. Nevertheless nothing could dampen the enthusiasm and excitement of the community. Despite the fact that the mission was held in mid-winter, thousands and thousands of people braved the cold and poured into the city stadium for the opening and closing rallies.

It was only during the weeks before the events that Barbara Shepherd suddenly remembered the prophecy of 1972. This was indeed ten years later, and the city had never seen the like of it before. Some weeks later, Africa Enterprise hoped that a similar crusade might be held in Zimbabwe's second largest city, Bulawayo. They asked me to accompany them down there and share information with the pastors of that city about our own crusade. I was able to tell them of one incredible miracle that had happened. On one of the first visits of the Africa Enterprise 'set-up' team, led by David Richardson, he had shocked us rigid by telling us that we would have to raise all the local expenses, which he anticipated at that time would be $13,000. Most of our Churches were unable to pay their pastors a full-time wage, let alone raise that kind of money. But, after much anguish, the Ministers' Fraternal as a whole decided that we just had to step out in faith and believe that God would provide the necessary resources. Within a week of making the decision to go ahead – and long before we had had time to plan a

campaign for funds from among our respective Churches –
we received an anonymous donation of \$11,000! As I ex-
plained to the Bulawayo people, it was like a confirmatory
sign from God that everything would be taken care of. In fact,
because the mission was far more extensive than we had at
first planned, and because the costs of a six-month follow-up
programme of literature for six thousand converts was way
beyond our planned expectations, the final overall cost of the
mission to the Ministers' Fraternal was over \$30,000! Not a
cent was owing when we finalised our accounts after the
mission!

A small group of Anglican ladies in Bulawayo then shared
a 'picture' with us that they had been given a couple of years
before, which seemed to be a confirmation of the 1972
prophecy. The 'picture' they had seen had been a map of
Zimbabwe. At one point on the map that corresponded with
Mutare on the eastern border, they saw an enormous shoal of
fish pouring out and spreading out all over Zimbabwe,
overflowing our borders into the countries on all sides of us.
Much of that promise seems to have been borne out by our
experience. Large numbers of people from neighbouring
countries have come to Mutare for training and the city itself
is now a centre for mission work into the devastated areas of
Mozambique. Trained evangelists from Mutare have moved
to many parts of Zimbabwe, and to countries bordering on
Zimbabwe. Much work is being done in establishing new
churches in rural areas of Manicaland by teams of evangelists going out from Mutare. Despite the government policy of
setting up communist-type cells amongst the various age
groups of young children and teenagers to promote Marxist-
Leninist doctrines, large numbers of young people are giving
their lives to Christ, and there has been an unprecedented
growth in Scripture Union groups in secondary schools in the
area. The enthusiasm and dedication of these youngsters,
and other young people who have left school, has to be seen
to be believed. All night prayer and fasting is a regular
feature of their determination to storm the gates of hell and
win back the young for Christ! Even more inspiring than
their ardent young communist counterpart, they will be
found devoting every spare moment to working for the ex-

tension of Christ's Kingdom, using their well-thumbed Bibles as a powerful weapon, sharper than any two-edged sword (Heb. 4:12,13).

Under persecution and almost endless civil war, deprivation and hunger, the Christian Church is growing faster in Africa than almost anywhere else in the world. Much of that growth, just as in the 'House Church' movement in Western Europe and elsewhere, is taking place outside the traditional Churches – be it mainline or Pentecostal – possibly because these Churches have tended to become so bound by past tradition, or because of their unwillingness to change, to allow freer expressions of worship and manifestations of the gifts of the Spirit, and sometimes because they have ostracised or expelled from their ranks those who have had experiences which differ from their own.

One of the marks of the very early Church was the freedom with which the new converts – with relatively little training in terms of many modern 'theological requirements' – brought new people to Christ through their infectious enthusiasm and excitement. No doubt they made mistakes, and no doubt some of their 'theology' was occasionally 'off-beam', but such people often do more to bring people into the Kingdom of God than whole battalions of theologically sound, poker-faced churchgoers (except when turning apoplectic at some innovation) who do little more than warm the seats of their pews on Sundays. One of the tragedies of the 'Mutare for Jesus' campaign was that nearly three thousand of those who made commitments for Jesus came from those who had some past connection with mainline Churches in Sakubva, a high-density suburb of the city. Although many of us offered to bring in teams to help these Churches in 'establishing' these new or renewed members, they said they were able to cope themselves. A follow-up exercise some months later revealed that most of those people never went to those Churches, but went into limbo or joined up with fervent 'fringe-group' Christians. The reason? By and large it was discovered that the only action these Churches took was to send Church councillors or elders to the people concerned. The visitors told them where to find their nearest church, gave them the times of services, and informed them of what they would be expected to give to the Church! The tragedy was that those Churches had few, if any, members who were able to nurture new-born babes in Christ.

TWENTY-TWO

POWER OF GOD IN LOVING THE BRETHREN

The coming together of teams of evangelists from different denominations served to underline other Scriptural principles of unity. No one can be happy about the divisions within the Body of Christ. All too often, in all too many places, the only time denominations show any concern for the sinfulness of their divisions is during times like the Week of Prayer for Christian Unity (18–25 January) each year, but it only seems to go skin-deep and is forgotten about, for all practical purposes, immediately afterwards. Instead of ecumenism, to most denominations it is still a case of 'you-come-inism' – join us, if you like, because we are the true Church.

Worse still is the open antagonism which exists between the leaders of many Churches in many areas. We know that all disunity is deeply wounding to Jesus. In one of the most moving prayers of Jesus' ever recorded, and prayed the night before He died, He spoke of the longing in His heart for all division to cease. It was a fact of life in the established (Jewish) Church of Jesus' day. There were groups that could not tolerate one another, or who 'looked down their noses' at one another, and the Jewish Church has split into many more groups since then. Jesus could also foresee it happening in the 'renewed' body that He had come to establish. And He cries out in that prayer:

Holy Father! Keep them safe by the power of Your Name, the Name you gave Me *so that they may be one* just as You and I are one . . . I pray not only for them, but also for those

who believe in Me because of their message. I pray that
they may *all be one*, Father! May they be in us, *just as* You
are in Me and I am in You. May they be one *so that the world
may believe* . . . (John 17:11b, 20–21).

There is an important principle about evangelism to be
found here. Until we are *seen* to be working together in unity,
the world will not believe. Nor will the world see the *glory of Jesus*.
I believe that is why so many interdenominational ministries
are seeing large numbers of converts being brought to Christ.
I believe that is why the 'House Church' phenomenon is
growing, expanding and developing large numbers of new
ministries while most of the mainline, and many Pentecostal,
Churches are losing numbers, and continually retrenching
men from the ministry. Those moving into the 'interdenominational' or 'non-denominational' or 'House Group' field
have given up hope of denominations coming together in any
kind of agreement – and many have pulled out of that kind of
'sectarianism' (the 'we're right and nothing is going to
change' syndrome) and linked themselves with those who
want to see God's Kingdom, and not denominational
empires, built up.

In the same way many would argue that the 'charismatic'
renewal, especially between the period 1965–80, had a pro-
found effect on the lives of countless thousands of people in
mainline Churches almost simultaneously all around the
world. Many had been nominal Christians before the Holy
Spirit changed their lives. Many looked for a greater freedom
in the Church's worship, particularly in freeing the Church
from much (as they saw it) of its dead formalism, and longing
to see everyone able to enter into worship by bringing
prophecies, Scriptures, testimonies, hymns and spiritual
songs to it. St Paul says:

This is what I mean, my brothers. When you meet for
worship, one person has a hymn, another a teaching,
another a revelation from God, another a message in
strange tongues, and still another the explanation of what
is said. *Everything must be of help to the Church*. If someone is
going to speak in strange tongues, two or three at the most

should speak, one after the other, and someone else must
explain what is being said . . . two or three who are given
God's message should speak, while the others are to judge
what they say. But if someone sitting in the meeting
receives a message from God, the one who is speaking
should stop. *All of you* may proclaim God's message, one by
one, *so that everyone will learn and be encouraged*. The gift of
proclaiming God's message should be under the speaker's
control, because God does not want us to be in disorder but
in harmony and peace (1 Cor. 14:26–33a).

The tragedy of the renewal was that it basically left the
denominations, and their traditional practices and formal
structures of worship, unchanged. Many lost heart. Many,
believing that 'their' Church would never change, moved out
and linked themselves with Church groups that were 'more
open to the leading of the spirit', and to patterns of worship
that allowed the full participation of the whole congregation
– under the direction and lead of the Holy Spirit – as
revealed, for instance, in the above directions laid down by St
Paul.

It was quite remarkable that the great strides made by the
Church as a whole in Mutare came about at those times
when the denominations demonstrated their unity and love
for one another – by sharing with, and learning from, their
varied patterns of worship; by getting alongside one another
and understanding why we believe this or that; and thereby
often broadening our own understanding of Scripture and
God's revelation to man; and even to the extent of not vying
with each other over each new convert, just so long as the
Kingdom of God was growing.

If we want to be with the Lord for ever, then there is a need
to love one another. 'If someone says he loves God, but hates
his brother, he is a liar. For he cannot love God, whom he has
not seen, if he does not love his brother, whom he has seen.
The command that Christ has given to us is this: whoever
loves God must love his brother also' (1 John 4:20,21). Of
course, many try to get round that challenge in Scripture by
saying that a 'heretic' is not a brother, thereby implying that
'our' Church has 'all' the truth; and therefore all other

Churches are not really a part of the true Body of Christ! What arrogance! Those who have adopted such a stance have made their denomination 'their God'.

To return to the Mutare for Jesus Crusade, one of the most positive things to come out of that was the desire of many of the denominations to work more closely together. Instead of being a group of Churches seen by the world as a group largely in competition with one another, there was a desire to be seen as a group that worked together in love – in order that the world may believe. In some ways that move was spearheaded by the lay people in our Churches. During the last three months of preparation leading up to the crusade, we had opened a 'Mutare for Jesus' office in the centre of the city. Every day that office was staffed by volunteers from many different Churches. We had batteries of typewriters, telephones and display boards, and by the time the crusade got under way, the pace was hectic. The office remained open for a couple of months after the mission to help cope with the mailing to six thousand people who had made decisions for Christ! At the end of it, the lay volunteer staff had developed such a wonderful spirit of friendship, and such a desire to continue working together for the Kingdom of God, that the Ministers' Fraternal were asked to keep open a 'joint office'.

However, the office we had was not really suitable as a counselling centre, so it was agreed that we should look for offices that would meet three important conditions: i) They must be on Main Street, and in the commercial area. (That alone seemed an impossibility because there were no shops vacant); ii) They must be at street level so that the general public would see them when walking by; and iii) They had to be large enough to provide for all the various ministries we thought would develop out of such a co-operative venture. In faith we closed down the first office, and began to pray for the right place.

Not long later, Duane Udd, the new pastor of the One Way Christian Centre, rushed into my house one day and said he thought the ideal place was about to come on the market. He had been into a very large photographic shop, with plenty of rooms and over 5,000 square feet of floor space, and they had told him that due to lack of business they were closing down.

We approached the estate agent who handled the property and could scarcely believe it when, soon afterwards, we were actually signing a long-term lease on the building. The agreed rental was $350 a month. In addition to two reasonably sized 'halls', which could be used for seminars and conferences, a third 'hall' was divided into sections, providing a large lock-up office for the tape library, an entrance foyer with chairs and tables for visitors, an 'office' section with desks, typewriters and duplicating machine, and also a 'tea and coffee' section. Furthermore, there were also other rooms which could be set aside for the prayer room (the central power-house of the complex), a book-lending library, storerooms and toilets!

A few months later we were in for another surprise – this time a totally unexpected bonus from the government. The new Rent Act on commercial premises had just been brought into being. Legislation made it impossible for landlords to increase rents over what was paid at a certain period the year before. Because our previous tenants had been facing considerable financial difficulties, the owners of the building had tried to help them by reducing the rent in the hope that they would eventually get on their feet again. Our 'new' rent was now legislated to be $185 per month and we received a refund for all the 'excess rent' we had paid! (The rent does increase each year, but even at the time of leaving Mutare in 1986 was still less than $300 a month!) What an answer to prayer those premises proved to be!

Over a period of time I had collected quite a large tape library, mainly teaching tapes from a large number of conferences and the like. I allowed many people to make use of it on a fairly haphazard basis. One day, feeling it could be put to much better use if properly organised, I approached one of my parishioners, Felicity Watkins. I could not have chosen a more dedicated and efficient person to undertake the task. She even visited a very large tape library in South Africa to get additional ideas for improving the library. When it was all catalogued, re-labelled (with master copies safely put away) and stored in well-designed racks in nice new lockable steel cupboards – together with a super catalogue for customers – I handed it over to 'Mutare for Jesus', to be used by anyone who needed it. Thanks to Felicity's excitement, interest and hard work, we began to get gifts of tapes from all over the world. One tape library in Queensland, Australia, was so impressed by what they heard of the tape library through a friend who visited it, that they sent us a complete set of their David Pawson's teaching tapes (over 750 in all) and thereby filled many of our own gaps in that series. Many international Christian visitors, on being shown round, were so impressed that when they got home they arranged for tapes to be sent to us. In no time at all we had over three thousand teaching and music tapes in the library for the people of Manicaland to borrow.

Another serious drawback in Zimbabwe is not only our lack of Christian literature, but also our inability to import it. This goes back to the days of Ian Smith's government and 'sanctions'. Christian literature was given very low priority, and so the import of Christian literature was severely cut back. Soon after Independence, with import restrictions getting progressively tighter, our own Christian Bookshop in Mutare was left with almost no allocation for the import of religious books. Virtually the only Christian literature that now comes into the bookshop from outside the country is made possible by monetary gifts from overseas being channelled to overseas publishers for the purchase of books, and these books arrive as 'free gifts' from the original donor. Not surprisingly, there is very little to buy. However, many of us had books on our shelves which we had read once or twice and were unlikely to need again. I asked everyone in our community to let us have anything they could spare so that we could establish a Christian lending library in 'Mutare for Jesus'. Once again we were wonderfully blessed by many gifts, and in the gifted people we had in Mutare. Bette Olsen, another member of my congregation, spent hundreds of hours with a team of helpers, cataloguing all the books, and handling the on-going business of operating a lending library.

The 'Mutare for Jesus' complex also became the centre for many teaching courses, seminars and the like. We used it as our base for the evangelism explosion clinic and for the on-going evangelistic outreach into the city. We also undertook clerical work for Churches that had no office equipment and produced bulletins and so on for their use. A small reference library was set up for pastors who had no reference books of their own. The staffing of 'Mutare for Jesus' was done entirely with volunteer staff. *No appeals were ever made for funds* to operate the 'Mutare for Jesus' complex, and *yet we never needed for anything*! Voluntary donations more than provided for all that we set out to do.

The beginning of our working together as a group of Churches in Mutare probably goes back to the first renewal weekend we held as an Anglican parish at an hotel in the Nyanga mountains in 1976. It was so talked about around the town that when we were planning our second one, some of the Pentecostals in the town asked if they might join us – as did a group of Roman Catholic charismatics. That, too, was a tremendous success, and helped us to learn more about each other. About that time one of our Anglicans bought a large property in the industrial sites on which to expand his business. Eric Carlsen, having sat on the fringe of the Church for a very long time, ('I don't want to get involved' syndrome), gave his life to the Lord around this period. The change that came over him was truly miraculous. Having been the kind of person who was totally repelled by any infectious enthusiasm over religion, he suddenly became one of the most infectious and enthusiastic Christians I have ever come across – and still remains so to this day. (He and Jeanette now have a large home that houses a Christian community). His whole life is lived for the Lord. His business is dedicated to the Lord. When we all attended a large renewal conference in Johannesburg, it was here that Eric became certain that God was calling him to set aside his new property investment as a centre where Christians of all denominations could meet together – as we had done at the hotel, and as we had done on an even larger scale in Johannesburg, with Christians of every denomination and colour meeting together in reconciliation, love and harmony.

Over the next few years this new multidenominational complex was wonderfully used in bringing the whole Body of Christ together. We held many gatherings of the whole body, when people would take part in 'a time of renewal' from

Friday evening through to Monday afternoon, whenever there was a Bank Holiday Monday. The only times when we did not meet were on Sunday morning and evening, when everyone was expected to attend their own Churches. Lunches, teas and suppers would be provided by groups of women from the different Churches right through the weekend. We were blessed with a wonderful key organiser for these events in Muriel Acott, who took care of registration, setting up the programme and speakers, musical groups, crèches and children's programmes. Supported by her band of helpers, she ensured everything ran smoothly, with everyone obtaining maximum benefit from their participation.

Because the complex was within the city boundaries, many people who might otherwise have been deterred by the expense (staying at an hotel), problems with transport out of town, or being unable to leave wife or husband at home for the weekend, were able to attend. Some difficulty was experienced later in the war when the city's fuel storage tanks were at risk from rockets, and special permission had to be obtained to get through road blocks set up to seal off that part of the industrial sites during curfew times.

Eric, by now one of my churchwardens, had great difficulty in keeping his enthusiasm for the Lord in check, and found the Anglican Church extremely restricting to someone who wanted to see so much more freedom in our worship, and a much greater freedom in the ministry of the laity. Eric also believed that the One Way Christian Centre, as it was now called, should be utilised much more fully. When a new pastor in town asked Eric if he could borrow chairs from the One Way Christian Centre for the 'church' that was now meeting in his own home, Eric immediately offered the use of One Way as a place of worship. Naturally enough it was snapped up! Also not surprisingly, and because of some deep hurts caused by people leaving a number of Churches to join the new 'One Way' Christian Church, the large majority of Churches felt that they could no longer use the centre as neutral territory for inter-church activities. Eric and a number of my leadership were amongst those who joined this new Church. To this day they have provided much of the key leadership in that Church, and a great healing took place about a year later between ourselves and this group. We have all worked together very closely ever since and probably to greater effect – as many of the lay people have developed wonderful ministries that probably would never have been possible under the restrictions imposed by the Anglican structures. And there can be no doubt of their being used mightily by the Lord in the building of His Kingdom. Deep and lasting friendships, and much sharing of 'team ministries', have developed between myself and many pastors who have served in Mutare.

For some years now God has led us to cancel all our Sunday evening denominational services on the last Sunday of each month. In place of it, the whole Body of Christ gathered together for a joint service of 'Celebration'. A roster was drawn up in which one pastor was given the responsibility of leading the worship, and another the ministry of preaching, at each service. Musicians from a number of Churches would get together for practices and to play together. We got to know people in all the different Churches, and a real love developed between us all. 'The brethren' taking part in these monthly celebrations certainly 'dwelt together in unity', with a love that superseded the doctrinal differences we might still have. We learnt to accept and respect one another despite those differences. Perhaps more than anything else, our willingness to share those differences helped to widen our understanding.

Each ministry operating out of 'Mutare for Jesus' had its own sub-committee made up of members of different Churches, with each sub-committee reporting to me as the person responsible to the city centre pastors for the administration of the complex. At the centre of everything at 'Mutare for Jesus' were the prayer support groups for the various ministries. There was also, I believe, a really 'key' group brought together by the Lord, representing a number of Churches, to specifically uphold the Churches, and all the priests and pastors, in sustained intercessory prayer. They were called upon to pray for the various programmes being undertaken, for various difficulties being experienced in any one or more of the Churches. They continued faithful in this for many years, meeting one afternoon a week virtually without a break for the whole period of time. For much of the time there were seven in the group – Claudia, Barbara, Jill, Betty, Ning, Vickie and Debbie – and the Lord laid on them a need to *fast and pray*. Each one took responsibility for one twenty-four hour period each week – and for more than two years a continuous unbroken fast was kept. I believe it was that kind of commitment to prayer and sacrifice, to be found in a number of parts of the city, that enabled us to see God working so mightily in our midst, and which explains why the brethren were able to dwell together in unity.

Only God, through His Spirit, could work the miracle of bringing together so many different groups of His people – usually separated by man-made walls of division – to experience such love and respect for one another. We praise His Name for what He has done, and continues to do, in bringing reconciliation and healing.

TWENTY-THREE

'GO AND SELL ALL THAT YOU HAVE . . .'

The contrast between the lack of enthusiasm with which I faced my return to the full-time ministry, and the excitement that filled every part of my being within a year of returning, couldn't have been more marked. The job-satisfaction far exceeded anything I had ever known before. I found myself given gifts that were not natural to me. If there had been any indecision at all, it was only as to whether I could remain within the Anglican Church. There, too, I was firmly convinced that whatever the cost, God was calling me to remain and witness to the change that He had brought about in my life. Over the past eleven years I have been able to share with many people the story of how God brought about that change, and to tell them how He could change their lives, too. I was to share this not only with Anglicans who had never understood what God was really offering them, but also with people in many other mainline Churches in Zimbabwe and in neighbouring countries. Many have come to this experience of being born again, and of receiving the empowering of the Holy Spirit.

With the coming of this wonderful change in my life, I now had no thought of leaving Mutare. It was a lovely city, surrounded by mountains in the most beautiful part of Zimbabwe. My predecessor had been there for nearly twenty years. As I talked with God on more than one occasion, I told Him how nice it would be if I could just stay there until He called me 'upstairs'. Surely He wouldn't mind, I would ask, even if I remained until my retirement? A matter of twenty-eight years?

In 1984, however, I came to believe God was telling me to leave. In fact, I believed I was required to be willing to give up everything I had become so attached to in Mutare: the congregation we dearly loved, and the deep and loving relationships we had with people across many denominations. There was also our six-bedroomed house which we shared with such joy with a constant flow of visitors from near and far. There had been the challenge and excitement of seeing a new diocese coming into being and beginning to spread its wings, and the privilege of being part of that experience. Now I was being called to give up the security in which I had come to trust (although until that moment I had not realised how important a part it played in my life): the assurance of a regular stipend, and a pension.

The rich man who met with Jesus in the Gospels was told to go and sell *everything he had* (because it was more important to him than almost anything else), and give to the poor. Then, said Jesus, you may 'come and follow me'. Nevertheless, how can one be expected to give up everything when one has a family to consider? At the time our son Andrew was starting on his 'A' levels at school, Diana was in her second year at secondary school, Lynne who was only three, and I had my wife Jill to support as well. As a result, I decided that the suggestion that I give up everything could not have come from God! But the easy way with which I had disposed of the thorny issue of putting my trust in that kind of security – just like the rich man in the Gospel – left a considerable unease in my spirit. It involved a similar principle to my not trusting God to provide the words for a sermon. I salved my conscience, for some time, by regularly asking my churchwardens, Giles Wakeling and Robert Rugge, whether they didn't think the time had come for me to move? It was a good way of 'chickening out'. I asked the same question of other leaders, members of the Church Council, and friends. Nothing pleased me more when each one responded, 'Of course not, John . . .'

A few months later it was decided that Jill and I should go to the United States as 'ambassadors' for our diocese and meet with the many people in our 'Companionship Diocese' of Massachusetts in New England. As our diocese was unable to afford such an expense, the parish most generously responded to the bishop's suggestion and paid for the trip as a gift to us for ten years' service. As they informed us of the gift, they jokingly added a 'condition' to that gift and one can see how all my questioning had begun to make some impression on them: 'In making this gift to you, we expect you to sign on for another ten years!'

Their gift made it possible for us to spend two months overseas. We were able to have our own holiday first in Israel, visiting the home of Jesus (the most memorable and heart-moving experience for both of us), before flying on to spend three weeks in New England, followed by three weeks in the United Kingdom on the way home. It was a truly wonderful experience. Bill and Liz Reynolds were kindness itself when they moved into our house and looked after the two girls while we were away. It was also a welcome break after all the anxiety and strain that had followed an earlier mass demonstration against the bishop early in 1985, when Tekere and his supporters had, on this occasion, taken over the diocesan offices.

However, on our return the issues had still not been resolved. I learnt that the leaders in the diocese were determined to go ahead and press charges against the leaders who had been in rebellion, and who were strongly supported by their political friend Edgar Tekere, the former cabinet minister of Mr Mugabe's. I felt I had to make my own position on the question of charges clear, as I believed that Scripture clearly tells us that we are not to take a brother to court. I also warned (despite whatever assurances to the contrary were given to them by some government ministers and officials) that I could not see Edgar Tekere allowing these leaders, whom he had so strongly supported all along, to be prosecuted. If they were determined on this action, I said that I believed even worse demonstrations would follow.

The demonstration took place as outlined at the very beginning of this book, and on a far worse scale than anyone could have predicted.

The major reason for the publicity given to this desecration of the cathedral was that this was not the first time that this type of tactic had been used. Similar, politically-motivated, pressure tactics had been used as a weapon against a number of denominations and Church leaders in the immediate past. It was for just these reasons that both the Mutare Ministers' Fraternal and the Roman Catholic Justice and Peace Commission also came out with strong statements supporting our cry to the government to put a stop to this kind of political thuggery and intimidation.

After the invasion of the cathedral we spent a fortnight away from our home. A week after our return, Diana was rushed into hospital for an emergency appendix operation, but made a speedy recovery. Two days later a very senior member of the party telephoned me about the publicity that had been given to the event overseas, and promised that I would be severely dealt with by the party for bringing the country into disrepute (as he described it). The next morning a gang of thugs was waiting to ambush me near my office. I had had a dream the night before that warned me of impending danger, and I escaped with seconds to spare. Strangely enough two different people were, that very morning in their quiet time, given the story of St Paul having to escape those who plotted to kill him by being let down over the city walls of Damascus in a basket. The people given that reading, without having any knowledge of what was happening to me at the time, felt quite clearly that God was telling them that the story was for me. They shared it at a special meeting which was called that night.

As the family left for Harare on indefinite leave a few days later, we discovered that God had begun to do a wonderful work in us, as each one realised that we no longer had any concern in our hearts, even if we were never to see any of our possessions again. It was almost as if God had taken away our dependence and trust on such things. We spent six weeks in Harare living in many different Christian homes to avoid being found and we were quite wonderfully loved and cared for by the wider Christian community.

What came out of that stay was that we became increasingly certain that God was calling us out of the Anglican Church in Zimbabwe, and out of the country we perhaps loved too much. A whole range of prophecies was given to us, through many different people, all of them dovetailing together, and providing plenty of confirmation for each decision that was made. 'All things work together for good . . .'? Well, if there was no other way of getting me to let go of all the things I had been trusting in, then God could use the prevailing circumstances I found myself in to make it impossible for me *not* to resign. Now I would really have to start trusting in Him for everything.

Although peace was eventually restored between members of the party and the leadership of the Church, and an agreement arrived at with those who had been in rebellion, part of that agreement led to the appointment of the Head of the Witchdoctors' Association in Zimbabwe as Chairman of the Board of Governors of one of our most prestigious Anglican schools. It appeared to me, and still does, that Scripture clearly points out that God's people can have nothing to do with 'supporting' things clearly shown to be contrary to the Word of God:

> When you come into the land that the Lord your God is giving you, don't follow the disgusting practices of the nations that are there . . . don't let your people practise divination or look for omens or use spells or charms, and don't let them consult the spirits of the dead [*all* the things that the witch-doctors do]. The Lord your God hates people who do these disgusting things . . . Be completely faithful to the Lord (Deut. 18:9–12).

> Fear the Lord your God and worship only Him, and make your promises in His Name alone. Do not worship other gods, any of the gods of the people around you. If you do worship other gods, the Lord's anger will come against you like fire and will destroy you completely, because the Lord your God, who is present with you, tolerates no rivals (Deut. 6:13–15).

The New Testament is equally clear on what the Church's stance should be on this matter:

> Many of the believers came, publicly admitting and revealing what they had done. Many of those who had

practised magic brought their books together and burnt them in public. They added up the price of the books, and the total came to fifty thousand silver coins. In this powerful way the Word of the Lord kept spreading and growing stronger (Acts 19:18–20).

As a matter of conscience I handed in my resignation to Bishop Elijah when it became clear that the decision to appoint the Head of the Witchdoctors' Association would not be reversed. My resignation was accepted.

That resignation meant that I no longer had the security of a job or a salary. I would also be without a house and car, and would lose my pension. Furthermore, given government regulations, we would be able to leave the country with less than £400 to start a new life. It is possible to export some furniture and one's personal belongings, but at a cost of $700 a cubic metre! Not that the government is wholly to blame. On leaving the country many people (going right back to the time of Ian Smith's Unilateral Declaration of Independence in 1965) had done everything possible to get round regulations and exported far more than was permitted. The net result was that those who followed later faced tighter and stricter controls, and were allowed to take out less and less. Another problem which resulted from my resignation was being able to raise most of the cost of the air fares for the family to travel to England. All these factors were known to us when I faced the consequences of resigning. It was a choice we freely made. We accepted it because we believed God was calling us to move to England.

There was no way we could pay for those air fares *and* export our furniture. Apart from anything else, we did not believe we could in conscience spend considerably more than the furniture was worth in exporting it. We had virtually no savings, so we decided to sell all our furniture and many of our possessions, and used the money to pay for the fares, and to cover the cost of sending a limited amount of clothing, crockery, cutlery, linen, bedding and kitchenware by sea. That way we would at least have something with which to start a new home . . . eventually! The small life policies we had were cashed in and the money given to further the work of God in Mutare. What was refunded to us from a recently established Zimbabwean Pension Fund for the clergy provided the whole family with a wonderful holiday around Zimbabwe just before we left in July, 1986.

I was warned by an old friend and former bishop, Paul Burrough (recently retired in England) that the prospect of getting a post in the Church of England could be difficult, as the Church Commissioners still required the number of posts presently filled to be reduced. Bishop Paul was of great support during this time, writing us many letters of encouragement and helpful advice. He had been 'through the mill' himself before leaving Zimbabwe some years earlier, also at the hands of Edgar Tekere.

The decision to give up everything was probably the hardest decision I had taken in my life. To surrender everything I knew, and hand in my resignation. For what? An empty future? And what about providing for my family? Yet, over and over again, during that period of exile in Harare, God showed us in our daily Scriptures (and in many of the prophecies given to us) that He would take care of our every need. All that was required of us (so easy to say, so difficult to obey) was that we entrust ourselves and our future to Him, and step out in faith.

There was one further complication. I believed that I could get a job in bookkeeping or administration, but we were convinced (and again this was borne out by prophecy) that God was saying to me that I was *not* to take a job of any sort for some time (six months to a year seemed to be the time span) because He wanted me to deepen my relationship with Him. Like so many in the ministry, my life had been so hectic working *for* God in the past ten years, that my relationship *with* Him was not all that it could be. Perhaps it was David Watson's book *Fear No Evil* that had started this train of thought in me. Our work *for* God becomes so important in our eyes. Yet what God wants for us more than *anything* else is to just spend time *with Him*, alone. That, to Him, is as precious as it is to any two people deeply in love with each other. How fantastic! To realise that the God of this universe calls you and me into an individual, *personal* love-relationship with Him. Unbelievable! But how does one go to a new country with less than £400 in one's pocket, a family to provide for, no home that one can call one's own, and not work for a considerable period of time while one spends that time with the Lord?

God's clear answer to me was, 'Trust Me!'

We took that leap of faith. By the time we left Zimbabwe, I had had almost nothing to do for over four months except spend a lot of time with Him – and I have never heard Him speak to me so much before, or so clearly. I was also able to hand over all the responsibilities I had been carrying, and sell up everything.

For years I had handled all the administration of the diocesan trust funds on behalf of my fellow trustees. This covered funds held for the diocese, for parishes, and for missions – together with all the property of the diocese. It also involved the handling of many grants from overseas for specific projects – involving detailed applications, costing, and financial returns to donors and donor agencies. I also had the responsibility for the profitable investment of those funds. As I handed over that responsibility, and the other trustees signed for all the assets together with the audited accounts, a marvellous sense of peace flooded through my being.

My life as dean of the cathedral parish, my primary task, had also been a very full one, and immensely satisfying and encouraging – as this account probably reveals. However, even as I handed over that task, there was the assurance that God had no more for me to do there, and that others had their part to play in bringing all God's people to their full stature in Christ. The Cathedral Church Council had always been very understanding about my deep commitment to working with all the Churches, and to working outside the Body of Christ to bring the lost into the Kingdom. Whether I was travelling away to hold evangelism clinics, attend and teach at renewal conferences, or work on joint Church projects in Mutare and in the wider Church, they generously allowed me complete freedom to act according to what I believed God's priorities for my time should be. Never once was there any suggestion that, because they paid my salary, all my time should be spent only on those 'who footed the bill'.

There was also a sense of shedding another load as I handed in my resignation as Chairman of the Ministers' Fraternal, and handed over – something that had become especially dear to my heart – all my responsibilities for the administration of the 'Mutare for Jesus' complex.

It was like having an incredible load lifted off one's shoulders as I released one job after another. Of course, one never really appreciates the load until that point, because it is something that has been gradually increasing over a period of time. It's like the analogy that was once told me about the frog. Put in a beaker of water over a flame, he doesn't realise how critical his situation is; for as the water temperature rises, his body adjusts to it. Only too late does he realise (if he realises it at all) that he has reached the critical point of no return! Similarly, it was only as I was freed of all these responsibilities that I realised what a weight they took off my shoulders, and I began to understand my family's complaint that I was a 'workaholic'. Those four months were one of the most wonderful periods in our life as a family. We had never seen so much of each other *as a family*, and we enjoyed it immensely.

It was not that I hadn't enjoyed doing all the jobs that I had taken on. I had done so, tremendously. Naturally there were heartaches at saying farewell to those we loved so deeply, and many a tear. Even so, we felt deep peace about our decision because we shared the belief with those close to us that this was of the Lord, and that even if we did not meet up again in this life, we would soon be together again for ever.

As the day of our departure drew nearer we felt, understandably enough, some concern about our future means of support. We started to joke with friends that if nothing else materialised, we might be reduced to seeking shelter under the Severn Bridge! Not surprisingly our parents and other members of our extended family felt that it might have been wiser to have had a job lined up before venturing into the unknown in another country. Many of our Christian friends, because of their love and concern for us, also couldn't help but express some anxiety from time to time. We had to keep reminding ourselves that Jesus did indeed say, 'Take no thought for the morrow' . . . 'Your Father knows you have need of these things' . . . 'food, clothing, drink.' The priority Jesus lays before us is crystal clear: 'Seek ye *first* the Kingdom of God', and *then* all these things (food, drink, clothing, jobs, homes, security and so on) will be added to you!

It was only *after* we stepped out in faith and *cut all our ties* – and only then on the very eve of our departure – that we received an unbelievable offer.

TWENTY-FOUR

'BEHOLD I MAKE ALL THINGS NEW'

The unbelievable offer came from a Christian Fellowship in Theydon Bois in Essex, England. They had heard of our difficulties and trials through mutual friends. We knew nothing of the Fellowship at that time, nor had we ever heard of Theydon Bois before. (It's a little village just outside the north-east border of Greater London with a population of about 4,500, and maintains its village character by refusing to have street lights.) These people had been led to pray for us, with the leadership being convinced God was calling on them to provide for us. Through John and Jenny they telephoned a message to us to this effect, and followed it up with a confirmatory letter. The Fellowship is under the leadership of three men: Alan Mutter (Deputy Director of Education for Enfield in Middlesex) and his wife Barbara; Mike Steward (Professor of Immunology at London University) and his wife Lynn; and Vincent Wiffen (retired from local government) and his wife 'Jimmie' (Doris). What an unbelievable offer of Christian love, generosity and self-sacrifice to extend to an Anglican dean and a family they had never met!

In the confirmatory letter, each leader and his wife added a personal message. Amongst other things they said: 'We'll just put ourselves in God's hands and do anything He asks' . . . 'Whatever is ours is yours if you need it' . . . 'We would like to assure you that we have some accommodation available and will be very happy to share it with you for as long as you need it.' (Another strange coincidence in this story is that Alan and Barbara had been virtual life-long friends of the leaders of the Elim School at the time of the massacre.)

This offer of help was a wonderful answer to prayer, and an assurance to us that God was already taking care of our 'provision' in England. Very soon after this news was received, we had our final Celebration Service (gathering of all denominations in our monthly corporate act of worship) in Mutare. Although most certainly not planned as such – I had drawn up the roster of preachers for those monthly services nearly a year earlier – I was down to preach for that particular service! Duane Udd, who led the worship, also turned a part of the service into a moving farewell for the Knight family. The 'One Way Christian Centre', where this particular service was held and which held so many treasured memories for us, was packed to the doors. The whole congregation prayed over us, and I was so emotionally moved by their love and concern for us, that I found it very difficult to preach. Immediately before doing so I told them, knowing the concern many had for our future provision, that we had received this wonderfully comprehensive offer. I explained that we had agreed to go and stay with the Christian Fellowship for a short while after our arriving in England. This would be followed by a visit to Jill's brother and sister-in-law, Howard and Claire, in Duffield. Then the Fellowship would have time to decide – having met us – if they wanted to stand by their offer!

While I was telling the congregation about this unknown Fellowship, I had no idea that a young man was in the congregation, trying to summon up the courage to stand up, interrupt me, and tell the congregation that he knew the Fellowship, and the village of Theydon Bois, because he came from that part of England!

One can imagine the kind of odds a bookie would offer on the chances of a member of a tiny Fellowship in a very small village in England six thousand miles away, being in a particular church in a very small city in Africa, at the very moment the preacher mentioned that Fellowship by name! Mark had, earlier that day, been in Masvingo nearly two hundred miles away. (He knew nothing of me, or the offer that his Fellowship had made because he was already on holiday!) He had hitched a lift through to Mutare, and asked people he met there if there was a service he could attend that evening. He was brought to the place where we were meeting! Now that is what I call a God-incidence, rather than a coincidence. As he spoke with many of us after the service about the loving people we would find in the Fellowship at Theydon Bois, it seemed a final confirmation that this was God's way of telling us that *this* was His provision. There was no other way of explaining away all those God-incidences!

Early on Sunday morning, 13 July, 1986, we landed at Heathrow Airport in England and were met by 'Jimmie' and Vincent Wiffen, and by the same Mark we had so recently met in Mutare. A few hours later the same morning (we did land *very* early) we were welcomed by the members of the Fellowship at their time of worship. For over six months, at the time of writing, they have showered us with love, been ever thoughtful of our every need, ensured that we needed for nothing, and embraced us as an accepted part of a really warm, caring and close-knit family.

Very soon after our arrival, those with education expertise in the Fellowship set about finding a solution to Diana's schooling problems. Her final 'O' level year in Mutare had been shattered by an enforced four-month break from school, both during the two periods of exile from home, and during the time of packing up to leave Zimbabwe. Through expert help and advice, the authorities concerned in England have been kindness itself – from the Cambridge School Certificate Board responsible for people like Diana writing overseas examinations, right through to Davenant School Foundation in Loughton – next door to Theydon Bois. Staff at the school have gone out of their way to coach Diana, and help her in areas where her past schooling has been deficient. After an academic year spent in their Sixth Form, Diana will be sitting a new set of 'O' levels in June, 1987. Lynne, too, has been equally well catered for, and is very happy with the place that was found for her in the Theydon Bois Primary School.

'The group of believers was one in mind and heart. No one said any of his belongings was his own, but they all shared with one another everything they had' . . . 'there was no one in the group who was in need' (Acts 4:32–35). How wonderfully this Fellowship have lived that out in their daily lives, both with one another, and with us who have been made very much a part of the 'group of believers'. As we have spent time waiting on the Lord, renewing and deepening our personal relationship with Him, and allowing members of the Fellowship to minister healing to many hurts and scars that had inevitably been caused in recent times, we have tried to live one day at a time, *endeavouring* not to be anxious for anything.

The greatest sacrifice was inevitably made by 'Jimmie' and Vincent, for it was their home that we invaded for nearly six months. They took us in and shared everything with us – not as lodgers or tenants, but as one would in a close-knit family. They were always there to pick up the pieces, to pray with us and for us, and to minister to our needs for healing. They were the ones who broke us in gently as we became accustomed to living in a new country (for most of the family), with its many cultural and practical differences. When I got down to writing this book, they made over their caravan to me as an office, so that I could work for hours on end undisturbed. Even after obtaining a small flat for us to live in – almost exactly six months after our arrival – they remain very much a part of the family. Villagers are still seen to raise eyebrows at Lynne calling 'Jimmie' and Vincent 'Granny and Grandpa'. But that is what they have become to us – family!

The Fellowship also discovered, even though I had spent so few years in England, that I was entitled to claim Supplementary Benefit. This indeed proved to be the case, and the DHSS (Department of Health and Social Security) provided much help as we set about re-establishing ourselves.

Times of worship in the Fellowship have often been something very special to us. The first impression that strikes every visitor is the warmth and love they have for everyone from the moment they begin to gather. No one remains a stranger for long. There are also many young people, especially people in their teens and twenties, thirties and forties. Many have musical ability, and use it in playing a wide range of musical instruments. There is a freshness and spontaneity – that admittedly doesn't *always* come off – to their worship, with many in the congregation bringing along to the service a reading from Scripture, a psalm, a hymn, a spiritual song, a prophecy, a tongue and an interpretation and so on. The leading of the Holy Spirit in all this becomes most noticeable when everything is seen to blend together, without any kind of prior planning or consultation before the service, and presents the worshipper with something that convicts him of God's presence, and of something that God is wanting to say to each individual that is relevant to his life at that time. There is a wealth of experience in this Fellowship, for quite a number have come out of leadership roles in mainstream Churches, and have previously served those Churches as preachers, elders and so on. They are also drawing in people with no previous Church background. All the preaching I have listened to has been of a very high standard, deeply challenging, instructive, encouraging, and very soundly based on Scripture. More than anything else, and I have experienced this myself as an occasional preacher, one recognises God's inspiration when the preached word dovetails in so perfectly with all that the others have brought, and with its relevance to prophecies, tongues and interpretations, that have been given by others during the service under the leadership of the Holy Spirit.

A strong argument is sometimes put forward by people outside the Fellowship that those who have moved out of other Churches would have done better to have remained there and worked for change within those congregations. I have been privileged to listen to the stories of many people in this and other fellowships. As with reformers of every age, one hears of agonising and very painful decisions that many have felt led by God to make. Many forget, or fail to appreciate, that such decisions *are* costly and painful. A decision of this kind inevitably leads to ostracism, ridicule, and even persecution from former friends, neighbours and colleagues. In a small community that is a devastating blow to a family – to be cut off like a leper of biblical times. Many knew that that would be the price. Some took that step despite the cost, because in conscience they believed God required them to make a stand for truth. Others were expelled from their Churches, as were Luther and so many others in history.

It was the *Church Times*, in its report on a meeting between Anglican Evangelicals and the House Church Movement, that said the renewal movements had to be seen as a vote of no confidence in the traditional Church. At that same meeting Dr John Stott is quoted as saying, 'we belong together in the body of Christ' and that 'a lot of our divisions are due to caricatures we have of one another' (*Church Times*, 23/1/87). We ignore at our peril the challenge of such movements and what they are saying to us in the traditional Church. There is a need to get alongside and discover why so many good people in leadership have left, and why they are attracting new members and we, on the whole, are not.

In the days of Jesus the Jewish Church, established and built by God, no longer moved with God despite continually going through all the rituals, ceremonies and forms of initiation. So Jesus Himself rebelled and established something new: a Church that *would* move on with God under the direct and observable leadership of the Holy Spirit, and testified to by the miracles, signs and wonders that followed.

During November, 1986, I applied for a number of posts with para-church organisations. The *reluctant priest* all over again? Yes! There *was* much that I found difficulty with in my Church. The fact that I was made the scapegoat for other people's problems and mistakes had caused much hurt; but God has been good and enabled me to forgive those who did that, and healing was given to each member of our family. What really has caused me concern, particularly on the part of so many in leadership, is the lack of belief in miracles (both in Scripture and in the present); the lack of belief in much of Scripture as the Word of God; the denial of the unequivocal evidence in Scripture for the bodily Resurrection and Virgin Birth of Jesus and so on; the denial of the operation of many of the gifts of the Spirit in the twentieth century – and the ascribing of some of those gifts to the work of Satan; the failure to preach the Gospel in many Churches, with services that are 'dead', because the work of the Person of the Holy Spirit has been deliberately restrained. So much of this points to the very grave danger that 'Reason' has become the new *god* of this age (the glorification of man's intellectual abilities). The Anglican Church has generally taught that truth is determined on three bases – Scripture, Tradition and Reason. Many of today's so-called *avant garde* theologians give 'Reason' priority over the other two. All too many people in the leadership of the Church today seem to have overlooked our roots – for both the Book of Common Prayer and the Thirty-Nine Articles stress over and over again that *Scripture alone* is the fundamental base on which ALL truth is to be determined.

So in seeking a job outside the Church was I simply trying to find something more acceptable to me? This became clear to me in the interviews that I attended. I felt decidedly uncomfortable each time I was asked the reason for leaving the full-time ministry. Although I could talk about a possible Pauline 'tent ministry' (Paul was proud to earn his keep making tents while continuing his missionary work) I felt an unease in my spirit, because at this point in time I could not see a part-time ministry being more effective than the full-time one I had had in the past.

All denominations are imperfect, and their members are imperfect. As a Christian sticker has it, 'I'm not perfect; but be patient, God hasn't finished with me yet'! This was also made clear to me by two other things that I observed. Close friends were very unhappy in a lifeless Church where the Gospel was not preached, and the priest antagonistic to renewal. Although they would love to have looked for a Church that would meet their needs and 'make them happy', they were brought up short with: 'How can we leave when so many in *this* congregation don't know Jesus as Lord and Saviour?'

The other thing concerned Sid Freeman, a member of the Fellowship. He had the seemingly impossible job of promoting Scripture in an atheistic environment, but instead of looking for a more congenial area to work in, each week he asked for prayer to remain faithful to the Gospel where he was, whatever the apparent odds against his team!

The Fellowship has been much involved in praying for our future ministry in England. When they said 'Come and stay, no strings attached', they meant just that. They were delighted when I said I believed God was calling me back into full-time ministry and that we were going to knock on the doors of the Church of England. So were the Anglicans we had come to know and love in the area, particularly at Coopersale where I had preached and ministered. Ralph Harding (the vicar) and his wife Elizabeth, who have so loved and supported us, were particularly thrilled.

Whether the door is opened for us to continue ministry in the Church of England, or whether God has some other full-time ministry in the wider Church, waits to be seen. We seek only to be obedient to God's will and purpose for our lives. The truly astounding truth is that nothing happens by chance and, as the Psalmist says: 'the days allotted to me had all been recorded in your book, before any of them ever began' (Ps. 139:16). 'I chose you before I gave you life, and before you were born I selected you to be a prophet to the nations' (Jer. 1:5). And that is true of everyone God calls into His service. His plan for each of us is perfect!

At about the time we were reaching these conclusions, a word was shared with us in one of our times of worship – through Sandra Walker – which I felt spoke specifically to me and my family in our situation:

Driving along to work one morning, I was overcome by the sheer beauty of the trees in their autumn colours. I could not comprehend how God could create the many different shades of colour, and blend them all so well together. But then I felt a sense of sadness as the leaves began to flutter from the trees, and I was aware of the fact that soon the trees would be bare and unlovely.

Then I remembered God's promise of new life, and it would all come alive again. God spoke through that picture and said, 'When you reach an autumn in your lives, and your leaves begin to fall, remember my promise. When all seems to be going wrong and life loses its colour, and piece by piece it crumbles and falls away, take hold of my promise: "I will never leave you nor forsake you", but put your hand in mine and I will reclothe you again. Spring will come to you again, and will give colour and beauty to your life . . .

As the wind blows through the leaves and they flutter to the ground, I will blow my Spirit through you and all your unrighteousness will flutter away, and my Spirit will reclothe you in a new and wonderful way. Reach out now and let my Spirit blow in, through and over you until you are completely immersed in my love.'

Some of the seemingly cataclysmic events of recent times have indeed led us to 'an autumn' in our lives. Yet having experienced so much of this miracle-working God over recent years, and having seen the abundant outpouring of His Spirit on individuals, congregations and situations, bringing about startling and exciting changes – quite literally 'rain in a dry land' (Hosea 14:5) – we are absolutely convinced of His promise for the future:

'Behold, I make all things new'!

EPILOGUE

Time after time I hear people say to me,
'Why don't we see miracles like there used to be?'
I still believe in miracles, God gives us when we pray,
For God is God like yesterday, and God is God today!
Chorus: God can do it again and again and again!
  He's the same God today, as He always has been.
  Yesterday, now, forever He's always the same,
  There's no reason to doubt God can do it again!

The complete version of this song may be found in *Songifts* (Ed. Jeanne
Harper, Hodder & Stoughton 1986) and is used with permission.